"M3 Ministries is one of the great e........ .... apos-
tolates in the Catholic Church today. In this book, diocese and
parish leaders will find the help they need to discern their first
steps in transforming the life of a parish."
—**Bobby Vidal,** associate director of evangelization, Office of
the New Evangelization, Archdiocese of Los Angeles

"As the Catholic Church continues to take seriously Pope Francis' call to foster communities of missionary disciples, this book
is essential reading to help our parishes move from maintenance
into mission. Deacon Keith writes an accessible, engaging, and
practical resource peppered with Scripture and anecdotes drawn
from his vast experience."
—**Julianne Stanz,** director of Parish Life and Evangelization,
Diocese of Green Bay, Wisconsin

ABLAZE

+

5 ESSENTIAL PARADIGM SHIFTS FOR PARISH RENEWAL

+

DEACON KEITH STROHM

the WORD among us® press

Published by The Word Among Us Press
7115 Guilford Drive, Suite 100
Frederick, Maryland 21704
wau.org

23 22 21 20 19 1 2 3 4 5

ISBN: 978-1-59325-364-6
eISBN: 978-1-59325-284-7

Cover design by Faceout Studios
Interior design by Suzanne Earl

Library of Congress Control Number: 2019907533

Made and printed in the United States of America

To Ron Huntley, Fr. Simon Lobo, CC, Rob MacDowell, Fr. James Mallon, Dan O'Rourke, and Kate Robinson—for friendship, inspiration, and your enduring commitment to the truth that culture *matters.*

CONTENTS

PART THREE: MOVING FORWARD

Foreword

"What does this have to do with Confirmation?"

"Everything!" I, almost, kind of, yelled.

I wasn't proud of my reaction. The kid was really getting on my nerves—he had been for weeks. We were one month into the new Confirmation program that I had introduced at a parish I was pastoring when I was a young priest. I had changed the model from a classroom-based, information-delivery model to a dynamic, relational, and evangelistic program that spoke a great deal about a relationship with Jesus in the power of the Holy Spirit.

The kid in question was real, but on reflection I realized that he was more of a living, breathing reminder and symbol of the colossal failure of the Confirmation programs I had thus far experienced. He had zero interest in faith and the Church. His family came to Mass twice a year but would be highly offended if their Catholic credentials were ever questioned.

I had received complaints about the new program from some of the parents—that after all these weeks their teens had not yet memorized the seven gifts of the Holy Spirit. But my answer still stands. Confirmation has everything to do with living in a personal relationship with Jesus, in the power of the Holy Spirit, and in the midst of the Church. To be fair to this young theologian, however, he was also correct—at least based on what he had experienced. In his experience, in the experience of his family, and in the experience of the parish until that point, a personal relationship with Christ—and all that goes along with it—has absolutely nothing to do with Confirmation.

That initial attempt to transform a parish Confirmation program was a clear experience of culture eating strategy for breakfast. This phrase, attributed to the business and leadership guru Peter Drucker, has proven to be profoundly true in parishes and dioceses all over the world. It is one of the reasons that beautifully bound parish and diocesan strategic plans litter bookshelves all over the world and collect dust. However, as I once heard it said, if culture eats strategy for breakfast, leadership eats culture for lunch. Gastronomic metaphors aside, the point simply is that nothing shifts unless the culture shifts, but here's the thing: *it can be shifted*. Leaders shape culture consciously or unconsciously, by design or by neglect, through what is rewarded and what is tolerated, and to do anything by design simply means that it is done with intentionality.

I have known Deacon Keith Strohm for more than five years. He was and is a great friend of Saint Benedict Parish, and has spoken at several events and done staff retreats. He is also a great friend and supporter of Divine Renovation Ministry, as he leads parish missions throughout the world that are connected with Divine Renovation and also helps to edit our books. Deacon Keith has years of experience working within parish and diocesan structures and is active in accompanying parishes and dioceses through M3 Ministries. I welcome this new book and I rejoice in yet another voice that speaks on the necessity of doing the groundwork in this challenging time in our Church.

Parish and diocesan renewal will never take place by simple tweaks or focusing on some "best practices" or programs. These practices need to be supported by plans and by strategies—and all strategies will be effective insofar as the underlying culture supports it. *Ablaze* gets to the heart of the matter in challenging parish and diocesan leadership to step up and, in spite of the cost, lead a transformation of the culture of their organizations.

Read this book, pray, and discuss. Let us change our conversations and the conversations in our parishes and diocesan board rooms. Let us change the conversation in the Church because when the conversation shifts, so does the culture.

If we get this right, perhaps fewer young priests will experience frustrating conversations with young, frustrated confirmandi.

Fr. James Mallon
Author of *Divine Renovation: Bringing
Your Parish from Maintenance to Mission*
June 21, 2019
Halifax, Nova Scotia, Canada

Introduction

"Why do you keep doing this to me, God?" I yelled from the confines of my Honda Civic, which was stuck in heavy Chicago traffic.

The frustration and anger were very real but had little to do with the intense congestion on I-90. I had just finished a retreat for the parish council of a Chicago Catholic church. Fewer parishioners were engaging in the life of the parish, and the council had asked me to help them address this issue. I understood that lack of engagement was likely the result of a deeper, more systemic problem, one that would require more work than a three-hour retreat. Nevertheless, I had hoped that we could lay a good foundation on which to build a comprehensive response.

For twenty years, I have worked with (and within) parishes to bring about renewal. For the past two years, I've worked full-time as the executive director of M3 Ministries. I knew from experience that the concepts behind parish transformation—concepts such as evangelization, discipleship, accompaniment, and encounter—can be challenging for Catholic parishioners and leaders to integrate into their understanding of parish life. I also knew that I had to find creative ways to communicate those concepts, to help leaders grasp what was involved. With that in mind, I had spent a good deal of time the night before this retreat retooling my presentation and fine-tuning my language and approach. By the end of the night, I was confident that I had put together something that would bear fruit for this group.

Only to have that confidence shattered against the harsh wall of reality ten hours later. The parish council members I met that morning were intelligent, articulate, and deeply committed to the renewal of their parish. But within forty-five minutes of my first presentation, I could see by the looks on their faces that they were overwhelmed and somewhat lost. I made what corrections I could to my approach, we had some great discussions, and at the end of the day, these wonderful men and women expressed their gratitude as they saw me off. Clearly, however, I had had a minimal impact on this council.

Thus my shouting session with God. Frankly, I was tired of leaving people overwhelmed with information and confused. When it came to communicating with others about evangelization, mission, and discipleship, I sometimes felt as if I hailed from another planet and my universal translator device was broken. Things reached a fever pitch in my car when I finally shouted, "If you want me to continue doing this work, Lord, you are going to have to give me some help!"

And help he did.

As I navigated through the traffic jams and gridlock that are regular parts of life in Chicagoland, I began to see, by the grace of God, the root of my problem. A major reason for the confused looks people sometimes gave me, and their overwhelmed reactions, was the fact that I was asking them to make major shifts in their fundamental approach to ministry and parish life. On a practical level, I wasn't offering a comprehensive overview—a strategic way forward—that would help them accept and act on these concepts of parish transformation.

In the hour and a half it took me to make my way home from the parish council retreat, I reflected on my years of experience on the front lines of parish ministry. Sorting through those years, I gradually realized that five paradigms—or patterns—of thinking and behavior are typical of Catholic parish and diocesan life, and these paradigms restrict growth and renewal. In order to facilitate renewal, leaders must make five essential shifts in those patterns: moving from a paradigm of *institutional faith* to one of *intentional faith*; from a paradigm of *engagement* to one of *encounter*; from a paradigm of *maintenance* to one of *mission*; from a paradigm of *programs* to one of *people*; and from a paradigm of *avoidance* to one of *accountability*.

These can be seismic shifts. Just as earthquakes can change the landscape and geography around us, these paradigm shifts can radically transform a parish community.

I realized something else while reflecting on my experience— something critical. Leaders who are unable to make these shifts will be unable to help a parish on its path to renewal. Furthermore, *such leaders will actually be obstacles to transformation and renewal.*

My experience bears this out. We live in an amazing time in which the Church has more books, programs, conferences, and resources focused on evangelization and mission than we've ever had. And yet over and over, I have seen and heard of pastoral leaders and other Catholics who return to their parishes on fire to apply what they have learned—only to face opposition, misunderstanding, or lack of interest. Often, after the conference is finished, the book discussion group has ended, or the workshop is over, nothing happens. Even the most dedicated pastoral leaders struggle in the face of these realities. They don't know where to begin!

That's why I wrote this book. Perhaps you've been on an individual quest for knowledge about parish renewal, and you're eager to put what you've learned into practice—but you feel isolated and alone. Maybe you serve on your parish's pastoral or finance council, and you know that something needs to change, but you're not sure what. Maybe your parish staff has attended a conference or been through an extensive study of discipleship, evangelization, and parish renewal, and your pastor is on board and has assembled a team that will carry out a process of renewal. But you're having a hard time getting started, or you feel as if you are spinning your wheels and getting nowhere. In the pages of this book, you'll find easy-to-understand language about the concept of parish transformation, a solid foundation in the five essential paradigm shifts, and a simple process to start your parish on the journey to renewal and transformation.

It's challenging work to transform a parish into a vibrant community where the life-changing power of Jesus Christ and his mission of evangelization are front and center. In fact, it may be some of the most demanding work a parish will ever do. But the power of the Holy Spirit has been given to us so that our parishes can live out their identities as missionary communities in fruitful ways.

May your understanding of the five essential paradigm shifts presented here speed you on your way.

PART ONE

SETTING
THE
SCENE

1

Getting to the Root

When I was eleven, I tried my hand at gardening.

Growing up on Long Island, New York, near the border of Queens, we didn't own acres of property. However, there was a small patch of ground off to the side of our home where my parents sometimes grew tomatoes. I asked them if I could start a garden there, and they said yes. I dutifully set out turning over the earth, preparing the soil, and planting seeds. In a short time, I was delighted to see the first shoots of green poking out from underneath the dirt. I watched in fascination as life grew from this little plot of land.

That fascination soon turned to consternation and then horror as I noticed other things growing out of the ground—things that I had not planted and which threatened to overtake and choke out the vegetables that had started to emerge. I pulled those invading weeds, but no matter how hard or how often I yanked them out, they returned in the exact same spots. When I went to my parents for help, they explained that I had to reach deep into the soil and pull the weeds out by their roots to ensure that they wouldn't return.

Getting to the root: that's a life lesson that has stayed with me.

If you're reading this book, you're probably interested—at least on some level—in the transformation and renewal of your parish. Organizational change of any kind, however, poses serious challenges. The history of business in the United States, for example, is filled with the "corpses" of companies that, unable to navigate change, were beaten by their competitors or rendered obsolete by the marketplace. Leaders who *do* manage to transform their organizations tell stark stories of the difficulties that lie in wait for those who want to walk the path of renewal. Challenges to organizational change are heightened in the Church, where we recognize that it isn't merely a human institution but a divine reality with a living tradition and real teaching authority.

Missionary Mandate

Therefore, to begin this process of renewal and transformation in our parishes and to navigate the inevitable challenges ahead, it will help to reflect on the nature and purpose of the Church— to "get to the root" of her identity. I heard a story several years ago that offers some insight about this.

A mother had prepared a stack of fluffy and delicious-looking pancakes for her two young sons—William and John. Breakfast, usually a contentious time with a lot of shouting and crying, seemed to be going well. Both boys were smiling, laughing, and having a good time as they tucked into their food, until at last only one pancake remained. John, the younger of the two boys, reached out his arm and opened and closed his hand in the international toddler sign for "give me." William, a bit older than his brother and possessed of a much greater appetite, shook his head angrily. Stunned for a second by his brother's reaction, John began to shriek as only a toddler can. In response, William began to flail his arms and legs; sippy cups and plates went flying.

In the midst of this chaos, the mother spoke up. "Now, boys," she said, with a touch of iron in her voice, "it's times like this when we need to ask ourselves, 'What would Jesus do?' Don't you think that Jesus would give the last pancake to his brother?" John stared at his mother with a blank expression, but William broke into a beaming smile. "Mom, you're right," he said.

Then he whipped around to his brother and said, "Hey, John, you be Jesus!"

"You be Jesus!"

That's a call to the heart of every baptized man, woman, and child.

"You be Jesus!"

You be the Father's love incarnate in this world. You be the hands that reach out to those who are lost, alone, and suffering. You be the voice that speaks for those who have no voice. You be the heart that loves those whom society says are unlovable.

"You be Jesus."

This is the essential mission of the Church and the fundamental service that she offers to humanity—to be Christ for the world. We see this spelled out clearly in one of the foundational constitutions of the Church, *Lumen Gentium*, promulgated at the Second Vatican Council: "The Church, in Christ, is in the nature of a sacrament—a sign and instrument, that is, of communion with God and of unity among all men."[1] Citing other magisterial documents, the *Catechism of the Catholic Church* takes up this reflection:

> As sacrament, the Church is Christ's instrument. "She is taken up by him also as the instrument for the salvation of all," "the universal sacrament of salvation," by which Christ is "at once manifesting and actualizing the mystery of God's love for men." The Church "is the visible plan of God's love for humanity,"

because God desires "that the whole human race may become one People of God, form one Body of Christ, and be built up into one temple of the Holy Spirit."[2]

The language of sacramentality may surprise us. A simple way to understand the Church's identity is to look at one definition of sacrament: that it is "an outward and visible sign of an inward and invisible grace."[3] Jesus makes visible the Father's love—which is invisible to us—in a way that connects us with grace. And Christ's body, the Church, makes Jesus visible to a world that cannot easily see him. The Church, therefore, conveys to the world the very life of God, a life that he offers to all.

The Church has a name for this sharing of Jesus and the life he offers: evangelization. As has been pointed out in books like *Forming Intentional Disciples*, *Divine Renovation*, and *Rebuilt*, many Catholics struggle with the idea of evangelization, seeing it as a kind of spiritual telemarketing, a judgmental activity, or something that only our Protestant brothers and sisters do.[4]

The truth, however, is quite different.

In fact, Pope Paul VI identified evangelization as an essential component of the Church's life and activity: "Evangelizing is in fact the grace and vocation proper to the Church, her deepest identity. She exists in order to evangelize."[5] In other words, sharing Jesus with the world isn't just something the Church does but rather the heart of *who she is*—and this truth permeates every area of her life and mission.

The life and work of the Church is about more than providing social services, dealing with societal issues, passing on doctrine to the next generation, or even building community.

Rather, the heart of the Church is oriented toward *extending communion*—the communion that the Father, Son, and Holy Spirit experience among themselves. God invited humanity into this communion, and we rejected his invitation through sin, but the Father has restored us through the life, death, resurrection, and ascension of his Son, Jesus. In this communion, people receive healing, wholeness, and hope; they discover their deepest identity, their profound purpose, and their ultimate destiny. This reality is captured in Jesus' great commissioning of the Church, as he sent out his disciples to "make disciples of all nations, baptizing them in the name of the Father, and of the Son, and of the Holy Spirit, teaching them to observe all that I have commanded you" (Matthew 28:19-20).

Seeing ourselves through this lens reveals something quite profound. As members of the Church, you and I are not nameless, faceless cogs in a giant organization. We are not passive recipients. We are sons and daughters of God. He has called us specifically, and we have an integral role to play in the fulfillment of the Church's mission, each according to our vocation and state in life. If this is true of us as individuals, it is even truer of us in our common baptismal identity as the body of Christ within our communities of faith. Oriented outward, parishes therefore should be missionary outposts that release the love of God in Jesus Christ, touching and transforming individuals and the surrounding civic community through the power of the gospel.

There's just one issue: that doesn't seem to be happening.

ABLAZE

A Deeper Diagnosis

For a variety of reasons, Catholic parishes in North America have not embraced their identity as missionary outposts. Discomfort with evangelization, an historical emphasis on integrating the largely immigrant Catholic population into their surrounding communities, a rapid change of societal norms during the latter part of the twentieth century—all combined to bring us where we are today. The latest sociological studies make it clear that in North America and Europe, the Church is shrinking.

Again, many books, like *Forming Intentional Disciples*, have done a powerful job of highlighting those statistics and giving them context. We won't review them here because, frankly, we are living them firsthand. The average age of our parishioners is increasing; it's becoming harder to find volunteers; our leaders are retiring and not being replaced; and many of our children and grandchildren no longer practice their faith or even think of themselves as Catholic.

In this season of the Church's life, however, more and more Catholics, including Catholic leaders, are beginning to recognize the issues that we face both in the Church and in the world. According to our Tradition, there is a richness that is supposed to come from living a life rooted in Jesus—a richness stemming from the love, mercy, freedom, healing, and wholeness that Jesus offers. Yet the fact remains that many of our Catholic brothers and sisters have not experienced these things in their own life, and most don't even know that such richness and freedom are possibilities. As Sherry Weddell, cofounder of the Catherine of Siena Institute and author of *Forming Intentional Disciples*, has said, "There is a chasm between the Church's teaching . . . and Catholics' lived relationship with God."[6]

This chasm manifests in many ways, including lower attendance at Mass; declining participation in parish life; a lack of giving; fewer vocations to the priesthood, diaconate, religious life, and married life; passivity; and so on. Through God's grace, many parishes are beginning to recognize these issues and look at them with greater urgency. We agree that something must change. But what?

The truth is that many of the issues we currently face have plagued us for decades, and those of us who have been working in the Church during that time have struggled to solve these problems. We may have seen some success, but by and large our pastoral responses have not borne systemic and sustainable fruit. This isn't because we lack education, commitment, passion, experience, skill, or talent. It's because we have been reacting largely to symptoms and not to the fundamental "pathology"; our diagnosis of the issues over the last forty or fifty years has not gone deep enough.

For example, ever since I was a teenager, I have heard Catholic priests, lay ministers, volunteers, and deacons identify poor catechesis as a major issue in the Church's life. I would submit to you today that the Church has greatly improved its catechetical resources. And yet in ever increasing numbers, our young people continue to abandon any affiliation with the Catholic Church. There seems to be something fundamental that we have missed or been unable to put our finger on.

In many ways, it's like trying to steer an ocean liner around an iceberg. There are clear areas to avoid when you approach such a natural phenomenon: the tips of the iceberg. We know from the historical experience of the *Titanic*, however, that you can diligently avoid the tips of an iceberg and still run aground on a large volume of ice below the surface of the water. When I work with parishes and diocesan groups, I often ask them to describe what those "iceberg tips" might be in their own communities of faith, and then I overlay those things with a full image of an iceberg to demonstrate my point. You can see this in the figure on the following page.

We establish programs or processes—or we invest in events and resources—intended to deal with the tips of the iceberg, and then we're frustrated when that program doesn't change anything substantive. As pastoral leaders or deeply committed parishioners, we then try the next fix, and the next fix, and the next one, with an increasing sense of desperation.

For example, many parishes currently focus on getting their people engaged without giving them a deep understanding of the various dimensions of engagement. These parishes work hard to get people involved in things that happen at the parish: volunteering for events, liturgical ministries, committees, commissions, and so forth. Of course, there's nothing wrong with that, but it's possible to spend energy engaging people and simply converting them to the community, not to Jesus. And people often convert to the community as it exists at the moment of their conversion. So if the community changes—the liturgical expression changes, the pastor leaves, the school closes—these engaged parishioners are more likely to leave.

The problem is that we haven't penetrated to the root of the issue: the lack of discipleship. This is the base of the iceberg in

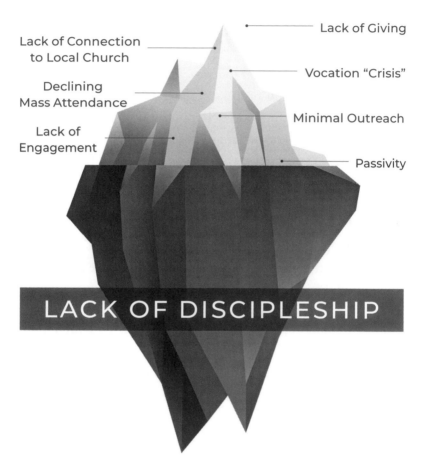

Lack of Giving

Lack of Connection
to Local Church

Vocation "Crisis"

Declining
Mass Attendance

Minimal Outreach

Lack of
Engagement

Passivity

LACK OF DISCIPLESHIP

the figure above; this is where we run aground. Our parishes and dioceses are filled with wonderful, loving, talented, and giving individuals *who are not yet disciples of Jesus Christ*. They have not yet made an intentional decision to follow Jesus in the midst of his Church. They have not embraced a life of active cooperation with the transformative power of grace that Jesus offers in union with his Father through the power of the Holy Spirit.

ABLAZE

Why have they not done this? Primarily because we, as pastoral leaders and involved parishioners, have failed to share the gospel message with them, inviting them to follow Jesus and walking with them on that journey. And we probably have not created structures and processes within our parish communities that nurture and reinforce that journey. In many cases, our people do not even know that an intimate, personal relationship with Christ—a union of love that can transform their life—is a possibility.

This crisis doesn't affect only parishioners. A lack of discipleship can be found among parish leadership, parish and diocesan staff, religious, deacons, priests, and even bishops. This is perhaps the greatest crisis in the Church today and the foundation of many of the issues we face.

We didn't arrive here overnight. The crisis of discipleship emerges from a confluence of systemic realities. As a result, there isn't any single silver bullet that we can aim at this problem, and the likelihood of a quick fix is abysmally low.

Then how can we tackle the problem?

"It's the Culture, Stupid!"

No, I'm not trying to be insulting. I'm drawing a comparison from the political life of the United States.

In 1992 then-governor Bill Clinton ran for president against the wildly popular incumbent, George H. W. Bush, whose approval numbers in March of 1991 were 89 percent. James Carville, a now-famous political operator and commentator, worked as the lead strategist on Clinton's campaign, and he knew that the road to the White House would be difficult. He created a sign that hung in Clinton's campaign headquarters, reminding everyone in the campaign that there were three simple messages they needed to focus on with laser-like precision. One of those messages read "It's the Economy, Stupid!"

Carville not only knew that George H.W. Bush and the Republican party were vulnerable on certain economic issues, but he also saw the economy as a fundamental reality that touched and influenced the life of every single American citizen. Winning that presidential election would require Bill Clinton's campaign to connect its message with this foundational reality and keep the attention of the American public there as well.

What does this have to do with parish transformation and renewal?

The change that this renewal demands is one of culture. Culture is the fundamental reality that touches and influences every facet of parish life. If we want our parishes to experience renewal, we must embrace new dimensions of what it means to be Catholic and what it means to be a pastoral leader in a mission-focused Church. Therefore this cultural change will be grounded in two major areas: personal conversion and pastoral or ministerial conversion.

Personal Conversion

Here's the radical truth: we are loved by a Father who has surrendered his Son Jesus so that we may be restored to relationship with God. Jesus invites every person to receive this new life he offers, and he asks us to surrender to him our sinfulness, our brokenness, our whole hearts—and to cooperate with the grace that he pours out in the sacraments and the life of the Church.

ABLAZE

Have we made this surrender? That's the key question for each of us. Have we made a deliberate choice to entrust ourselves to Jesus and to deepen that relationship in the midst of the Church?

Evangelization, discipleship, and the Church's mission cannot be understood from the outside. A truism of the spiritual life is *Nemo dat quod non habet*: one cannot give what one does not have. In other words, only a disciple can make a disciple. If we want to see our parishes come alive and bear sustainable fruit, we must first build up a generation of disciple leaders.

Pastoral Conversion

The heart of evangelization is accompaniment, opening our own life of discipleship to others and accompanying them as they walk into relationship with Jesus. Disciples are not mass-produced by programs. They are artisanal products, handcrafted by Jesus. The demands of the whole evangelization process—the making, maturing, and missioning of disciples of Jesus—will require us to rethink our fundamental approach to ministry.

That is, we must rethink how we understand, execute, and evaluate our identities, roles, and activities as pastoral leaders and rethink what it means to live as a parish (our culture). Quite often the skills and experience that we need in order to accomplish these things is not currently present within our current leadership and pastoral teams. We must commit ourselves to the formation that can equip us to bear fruit in terms of cultural change.

As you explore this book, you'll encounter information and resources to help you do precisely that. But, the best resources in the world cannot do the work for you. That's why many of us who are passionate about our parishes and the Church's mission often wonder if parishes can actually experience renewal.

I believe that's the wrong question to ask.

At the end of the day, the real question is not whether our parishes can be renewed and transformed. Of course they can. We belong to a God of restoration, healing, hope, and new life. Rather, these are the fundamental questions we should ask ourselves:

- Do we have the courage to take a different—perhaps radical—approach to living out our common baptismal vocation as communities of faith?
- Are we ready to change not only our activities but also our hearts and our identities in order to align with God's intention in creating and calling us?
- Are we ready to take an honest look at our communal models and self-understanding in order to embrace new paradigms that allow us to live as parishes in different and more fruitful ways?

I'm not advocating changes in the Church's teaching or innovation in the liturgy. I'm advocating a new approach to how we—parish communities who embrace a mission-centered identity in the twenty-first century—live out and apply the Church's teaching. If we truly want our parishes to be transformed, this is where revolution needs to happen.

Or as James Carville might say, *It's about culture, stupid!*

2

What Is Culture?

"When you talk about changing culture, I feel as if I'm trying to wrap my arms around air." "Isn't talking about culture really just touchy-feely stuff? When can we get to the important content?" "Frankly, I don't care about this culture thing. What I'm looking for is something concrete—an action plan—to help me transform my parish."

These are just some of the reactions I've received when I work with pastors and pastoral leaders on parish transformation. There's a sense that this "culture stuff" is a lot of airy nonsense, an excuse for business and pastoral consultants to bill the parish. At best it's secondary to the business of leadership, and at worst it's a major distraction from the actual work of parish transformation.

Nothing could be further from the truth.

Culture is not nebulous or theoretical; it has shape and substance. Edgar Schein, professor emeritus at the MIT Sloane School of Management and a world-renowned expert on organizational culture, defines culture as

> the accumulated shared learning of [a] group as it solves its problems of external adaptation and internal integration; which has worked well enough to be considered valid and, therefore, to be taught to new members as the correct way to perceive, think, feel, and behave in relation to those problems.[7]

ABLAZE

Now, that definition seems like a mouthful, but what Professor Schein highlights here is the close connection between culture and identity. As an organization or group interacts with the world around it, that organization begins to set boundaries, define itself, and place particular value on behaviors, actions, and types of thinking that are consistent with its self-definition and that bear fruit. This shared learning passes from generation to generation and becomes the lens through which an organization understands itself and the surrounding world. Members of the organization filter all actions, activities, thoughts, and behavior through that lens—*and they will modify behavior that doesn't fit within the established boundaries of their cultural understanding.*

The Power of Culture

Fr. Simon Lobo, CC, pastor of Saint Benedict Parish in Halifax, Nova Scotia, has a great deal of experience leading the cultural change and transformation of a parish. He initially served at Saint Benedict as an intern alongside then-pastor Fr. James Mallon and his senior leadership team. Fr. Lobo wrote about his experiences there in *Divine Renovation Apprentice: Learning to Lead a Disciple-Making Parish*. He describes the power of culture this way: "Culture . . . *becomes the environment in which ideas, strategies, and activities are analyzed, evaluated, celebrated, and, possibly, rejected.*"[8]

All organizations—including Catholic parishes and diocesan offices—have a culture. Catholic culture at the parish level influences the answers to questions such as, What does it mean to be a Catholic? What behaviors are associated with active Catholic life? How do Catholics communicate with each other and interact with non-Catholics? What approaches to renewing a parish are in line with Scripture and tradition?

Of course, there are concrete theological and canonical answers to many of these questions. Culture, though, acts like a lens through which we view everything. As Catholics we tend to see Scripture, Tradition, and things like canon law through the filter of culture, *privileging certain elements of those areas and downplaying or ignoring others.* Thus, many Catholics consider evangelization to be fundamentally Protestant, even as magisterial documents call out evangelization as an essential element of the Church's identity. There can be a disconnect between Catholic culture, as it is lived and experienced at the parish level by many Catholics, and the richness of our tradition.

For example, when I talk to Catholics about parish renewal and transformation, I try to demonstrate the influence of culture by throwing out a statement designed to violate a long-standing, almost unconsciously held value of Catholic culture. It goes something like this: "What if I told you that in order to renew your parishes, you will immediately have to stop the religious education of all children and focus exclusively on adults?"

I can hear the gasps, gulps, and teeth grinding from my audiences after I toss out that grenade. I make it clear that I'm not necessarily advocating such a strategy; I'm merely suggesting it as a possibility. But the shock and immediate resistance testify to the power of Catholic culture reacting against that possibility. For many parishioners, that approach just doesn't "feel" Catholic.

The fact is, though, that the fundamental mission of the Church isn't the religious education of young children but rather the making of disciples—and there are lots of ways to make disciples of children, including focusing on the discipling and formation of their parents first. As a response to the Reformation in Europe, the Catholic Church adopted a model of parochial education and formation that became part of the shared lived experience of Catholics through the centuries and therefore an "essential" part of Catholic parish life.

The power of our culture is such that even suggesting a change in that approach brings with it resistance. In some cases, our culture may cause us to reject certain possibilities and approaches as not being authentically Catholic—even if they are actually in harmony with Scripture and Tradition. Or even worse, our leaders may be unable to brainstorm new possibilities and approaches because our culture lacks the imaginative capacity to bring such ideas to light. We often express it this way: people don't know what they don't know. However, under the influence of the dominant parish culture, *it is entirely possible that people* can't *know what they don't know* without outside assistance.

The Difficulty of Changing a Culture

Understood in this way, it becomes clear that culture exerts tremendous power over concrete things like actions, decision making, processes, language, and investment of time and resources. I saw this over and over again in my almost fifteen years in the corporate world. Perhaps you have seen it as well.

The companies that I worked for frequently brought in consultants who led us in various exercises aimed at the development of a new corporate or business strategy. After working for days, and sometimes weeks, the group would produce a shiny new strategic plan, beautifully organized and collated within a binder and chock-full of colored charts, graphs, and illustrations. The first few times this happened, I remember being filled with excitement. At last, here was a solid plan for real change. But my hopes were dashed time and time again as that shiny new plan, filled with all the potential in the world, was placed on a shelf and essentially ignored.

The strategic plans themselves were fantastic. They were well researched, based upon solid data, and clear and concise in their approach to change. However, they failed to take into account the current organizational culture and the strength of what I call *cultural inertia*—the tendency of a culture to remain stable and unmoving in the face of pressure to change. In other words, the quality of a strategy, process, or program matters way less than the culture in which it is placed.

Think of the human immune system. When the immune system detects invasive organisms, it responds by producing antibodies to attack and overwhelm the invaders. The same is true within cultural systems. When an unrecognized thought, activity, or belief is introduced to that system, the culture moves swiftly to minimize, resist, attack, and ultimately drive out the "invader."

This is one of the reasons why a single silver bullet for parish transformation —one master program, event, or approach— doesn't exist. When we bring in a program, process, or event that contains cultural DNA different from the culture of our parish, the dominant parish culture reaches out to minimize the effect and fruitfulness of that program, process, or event.

Maybe you have experienced this in your own community. Parish leaders expend energy, time, and money finding the perfect *thing* that will turn around the parish and ignite a long-lasting transformation. They may even communicate to other leaders and engaged parishioners why bringing in Program X is so critical to the future of the parish. People nod their heads and never (or rarely) bring up any objections. Program X begins, and the people who come to everything join in, but the experience is too different, or doesn't seem Catholic, or asks them to see themselves and the parish in a new light. Some people complain to the pastor; most don't give any feedback at all to leadership but perhaps talk Program X down in private conversations with other parishioners.

As a result, Program X runs just a few times. There may be a slight blip in parish interest or engagement, but no long-lasting fruit emerges from the experience. Leadership meets and, seeing what has happened, concludes that Program X is not the solution. With a certain world-weariness, they go in search of the next program or process to bring in.

The cycle repeats.

This is why the work of M3 Ministries, the apostolate that I founded to help foster renewal and transformation in parishes and dioceses, proceeds from the following understanding: *all organizational change must pass through the door of culture.* If we try to walk the path of parish renewal without attending to the culture of our communities, we will simply be going through the motions, trapped on a treadmill of programming that bears few results. Or to appropriate the words of St. Paul in a different context, all of our efforts at parish transformation will become "a resounding gong or a clashing cymbal," simply noise (1 Corinthians 13:1).

In their book *Change the Culture, Change the Game*, Roger Connors and Tom Smith highlight the difference between motion and activity when talking about the importance of addressing cultural transformation:

> Ernest Hemingway once wrote, "Never mistake motion for action." Mere motion accomplishes nothing and can prove more exhausting than action. Energy expended without achieving the result can wear you out, both emotionally and physically. When it comes to culture change, we've seen far too many organizations just go through the motions, wasting time doing things that never yield any real change and progress.[9]

Does this sound like your experience of parish life? For many Catholics I encounter, it does. But it doesn't have to be this way. If we want to see real, lasting transformation and renewal, we will have to attend to our culture with the understanding that it is the cornerstone of our renewal efforts. Parishes will experience transformation to the degree that they are able, both through human agency and the grace of God, to transform the culture within those communities.

This cultural focus is not secondary to the activity of leadership or a distraction from the real work of change. It sits at the heart of parish transformation and is fundamental to the concerns of leaders. As human resource expert Michelle Crosby advises, coming to terms with the culture you have and the culture you want, and knowing that there are actually things you can do to move your culture from one place to another is every leader's job.[10]

Despite the difficulty of cultural change at the parish or diocesan level, it is absolutely possible—if leaders and key volunteers

- demonstrate a willingness to examine the current cultural realities that shape their communal life, experience, and ministry;
- choose new cultural realities that will move the parish toward the desired transformation; and
- focus on living those new realities out intentionally in every dimension of community life.

To do this, however, requires a deeper understanding of what makes up a culture.

The Building Blocks of Culture

In many ways, culture is like a living organism. And just as all life is built upon a cellular structure, cultures are made up of small, intertwined building blocks. To paraphrase Fr. James Mallon, author of *Divine Renovation*, our parish culture is the sum total of what we tolerate, allow, celebrate, reward, and punish. Another way to describe this would be to say, with Edgar Schein, that a culture "is a pattern or system of beliefs, values, and behavioral norms that come to be taken for granted as basic assumptions and eventually drop out of awareness."[11]

These beliefs, values, and norms (I'll call them *values* for clarity's sake) serve as the building blocks of culture. They are often deeply held by individuals, especially those in positions of authority within the organization, who reinforce them in rules, structures, and reward systems. As such, these values profoundly influence the way people act within an organization.

For example, I once worked as the director of marketing for a company that had modeled its culture around the Toyota Way, a system of management and operating principles created by the Toyota Motor Corporation. One of the fourteen key principles (or values) of the Toyota Way states that standardized tasks and processes are the foundation for continuous improvement and employee empowerment. This truly was a deeply held value at my company. I spent a great deal of time creating standard operating procedure (SOP) documents and holding my team accountable to both departmental and corporate SOPs. SOPs dominated much of my thought, my behavior, my leadership, and my language while I worked for that organization.

The values we embrace become second nature and are part of the basic assumptions that we make about our individual and communal identities. As such, they often drop off our radar and can have unintended consequences that we cannot discern, let alone understand.

Many years ago, I worked for a pastor who was a penny pincher; he saw this as a primary part of his leadership role. In order not to waste the parish's money, he instructed all staff members and groups using the parish office to turn on a light only in the room that they were using. As a result, much of the parish office remained dark throughout the day. The parish secretary talked to violators, or the pastor sent them a stern note. This went on long enough that visitors to that office often felt unwelcome or as if they were intruding. The value that my former pastor had unintendedly embraced, and effectively communicated to the rest of the community, was that *money was more important than people*. The lights in the parish office were one manifestation of that value at work. Unfortunately, manifestations of that value in other areas of parish life reinforced the very inhospitable fruit of that value.

When various deeply held values come together in a particular system or regular pattern, they strengthen one another, developing into a full-fledged culture over time. That's why it is so critically important to spend time understanding your parish's cultural values. You may find unintended consequences, such as those experienced under the direction of the penny-pinching pastor. When you understand your current cultural values, you can embrace ones that will lead toward renewal, transformation, and a fruitful missionary perspective. If you don't intentionally manage your parish culture, it can very easily end up managing you.[12]

Which leads us to our five paradigms.

A "paradigm," in common usage, is a worldview, a pattern of thinking, and a way of interpreting reality. In the context of parish transformation, think of the five paradigms as primary (or macro) cultural values that will wield the greatest influence over the life of a parish community—its actions, activities, and self-understanding. If we want to fruitfully participate in the process of transforming our parishes, then we as leaders must make an interior shift from the current paradigms we have inherited and embrace the five paradigms, or *major* values, that we will explore in this book.

The Secret Sauce

Much of the insight in this book comes not only from my experience working in parishes and dioceses but also from my work in the corporate world renewing brands, businesses, and companies. Some people recoil at the thought of applying business principles to parish life. "The Church is not a business," they say. "Therefore business principles have no place in the Church." On a certain level, they are correct. The Church isn't fundamentally a business. The mission of the Church isn't to maximize shareholder value year over year. The Church is a divine institution.

And yet the Church is made up of human persons, and therefore it is also a human institution. The Word of God chose solidarity with the human race. Jesus came not only to reveal God to humanity but to reveal humanity to itself, to show what it means to be authentically human. When we use leadership principles that foster what is truly human, we are indeed carrying on the work of the Lord.

Furthermore, St. Thomas Aquinas famously said that "grace builds on nature." When we dispose ourselves to cooperate with the grace freely given to us by God, the fruit of that cooperation results in freedom, healing, transformation, and renewal. The same is true of our communities of faith. In other words, if we cooperate with God's grace by applying organizational principles that promote healthy relationships, foster excellence, and prepare organizations for mission, we will see our parishes and dioceses set ablaze and radically transformed.

I had the opportunity to lead a staff retreat and a parish mission a few years ago at Saint Benedict in Halifax, when Fr. James

ABLAZE

Mallon was the pastor. After spending time with the community and its leaders, I saw that the "secret sauce" of the Divine Renovation model, the approach that makes it so fruitful, is that it combines the very best of human organizational leadership principles with a deep understanding of discipleship and deliberate cooperation with the supernatural dimensions of life in Christ.

Human receptivity surrendered to divine activity leads to dynamic change for individuals and communities of faith. Imagine what the Lord could do in, for, and through our parishes and dioceses if we could create cultures that foster such receptivity. The light of the gospel, the light of Christ, would blaze forth from our gathering places and shine into the darkest areas of human existence.

3

A Note on Vision and Mission Statements

Nothing clarifies the focus, energy, and efforts of an organization like well-crafted, well-used vision and mission statements. Like values, these statements can have a tremendous impact on culture. Understood and used in the right way, they are like a riverbed that guides and shapes the flow of water. Vision and mission statements direct a culture and give it form; they also provide clarity on the types of values a group should adopt in order to be fruitful in living out its mission.

Yet in my experience, parishes, corporations, and other organizations can spend an inordinate amount of time creating statements about vision and mission, but *the statements have little or no effect on the life and activity of that organization.* Many leaders, seeing this, have no use for such statements and consider them a waste of time. The disconnect between the importance of such statements and how leaders perceive them influences whether an organization will develop one and then actually use it.

The Difference between Vision and Mission

There is a difference between a vision statement and a mission statement, but this distinction is often lost. Here are quick breakdowns of both. (Note that the clearer you can be with your vision and mission statements, the more likely you will be to choose values that build a culture in support of your mission.)

Vision statements provide a clear sense of what the organization will be or will accomplish in the future, thereby describing what success looks like. In many ways, a vision statement answers the question "Where are we headed?" At their best, vision statements contain aspirational and inspirational elements. A vision statement is simple and brief, so that employees and members can memorize and repeat it easily.

For example, the Alzheimer's Association describes their vision as "a world without Alzheimer's."[13] This is a clear statement of purpose that is broad and inspiring, and their vision will guide their culture and decision making.

When working toward parish renewal, pastoral leaders should consider spelling out the community's vision. It should be broad and inspiring. Often our vision as pastoral leaders has been influenced by the difficulties we have experienced as we deal with fewer volunteers, smaller Mass attendance, less giving, and so on. Our vision has become too modest.

In working with a parish in the Midwest on leadership development and pastoral planning, I led several sessions on visioning. I tried to convince these leaders to dream big, but they always seemed to find reasons to limit their vision. Finally, after several meetings, they started to break free of their self-imposed bonds. Eventually they came up with this vision for their parish: "That everyone in our local community regularly gathers around the Eucharistic Table and goes forth spreading the Good News to all." That's right, they envisioned a time when everyone in their town would be in full communion with the Catholic Church, receiving the Eucharist, and living as missionary disciples. Now, that's a solid vision!

A Note on Vision and Mission Statements

Mission statements define the purpose of an organization and in a general sense answer the who, what, why, and how questions related to achieving its vision. These statements deal with the present realities of an organization and define its focus and scope. At their best, mission statements require only a sentence or two.

The Target Corporation defines its mission this way: "Our mission is to make Target your preferred shopping destination in all channels by delivering outstanding value, continuous innovation and exceptional guest experiences by consistently fulfilling our Expect More. Pay Less.® brand promise."[14] This statement is very precise. It's clear that the driving focus of the organization is outstanding value, innovation, and exceptional shopping experiences for their guests. This statement drives the decision making for Target.

The same should hold true when we develop mission statements for our parishes. The parish that developed the vision statement in my example above also created a mission statement that was clear and concise. They described their mission as a parish this way: "To hear and respond to Jesus' call to be his disciples and, nourished as a community by Word and Eucharist, to continue his redemptive mission of love and service to all." From this statement, we see that the community wants to focus on discipleship, growing in intimacy with Jesus through the Eucharist and the Scriptures, and sharing Jesus with the world.

Incarnating Vision and Mission

Unfortunately, there is often a gap between an organization's stated vision and mission and its lived ones. I once worked for a company that made a big deal about collaboration and even included it in their mission statement: "We are a company that acts collaboratively." Yet the management of that company did little to rein in several of its salespeople who struck out on their own, making promises to clients and receiving feedback that they never shared with their coworkers. In fact, those were always the salespeople who received the biggest commissions. But such a disconnect not only makes it hard for an organization to act with clarity and focus; it also fosters unrest, discontent, and dysfunction among the members of that organization.

The same is true in Catholic life. Several years ago, I had the opportunity to work with thirty or so parishes in a diocese on the West Coast. I was leading them through an exercise in which they analyzed the ministries and offerings of their parish. They were trying to identify whether those aspects of parish life specifically fostered the making of disciples, the growth and maturity of people who were already disciples, and the equipping of disciples to go out on mission. One parish team called me over because they were having trouble making the distinctions I had asked them to make. As one staff member put it, "Everything we do makes disciples." I asked them if making disciples was a part of their mission statement, and they said yes. I then asked them how many disciples their parish produced in the last twelve months. They looked back at me stunned and admitted that they didn't know.

That's an example of a stated value that has no actual bearing on the life of a parish community. If you talk about discipleship in your mission statement but don't even have a general idea of how many disciples your parish is producing, then that statement is simply talk. You don't actually focus on discipleship as a parish.

A Note on Vision and Mission Statements

In order to close the gap between vision, mission, and the actual life of your parish, here are some things to consider.

Simplify

Often multiple councils, committees, and commissions have a hand in creating vision and mission statements. As a result, every group has its own sacred cow or critical language that they want to include. Left unchecked, this can easily produce a bloated, complex statement full of buzzwords that mean very little to those who will try to live out this vision and mission. It will also practically guarantee that no one is able (or willing) to memorize it.

As you simplify your statement, identify the critical ideas and excise all the stuff that is "nice to have." In addition, look at any language that is present simply to provide a complete picture of Catholic thought or theology. It is impossible to summarize Catholic teaching in one or two sentences. if we wanted to catch the precision and nuance of our theology, those sentences would have to be massive and full of technical jargon. Remember, you want your people to be able to easily memorize and share the vision and mission statements.

Ten years ago, I led my own parish through a process of creating a mission statement. After quite a bit of time, we ended up with the following:

To spread the Gospel of Jesus Christ, offering people the means to eternal life in Jesus—through our sacramental life and our apostolic witness. To this end, we will form disciples and send every member out as an apostle to work for the transformation of our world—home, neighborhood, and workplace—through the power of the Holy Spirit.

I absolutely loved that mission statement. I truly was quite pleased with myself and the work that the leadership did to arrive at that statement—until we started having trouble getting the community to adopt or even understand it. In retrospect I can see that we should have radically shortened it to something like this: "To spread the gospel of Jesus Christ by forming missionary disciples through the power of the Holy Spirit." Of course, there would still be work to do educating and forming our people around missionary discipleship, but the statement itself would have been more approachable and user friendly.

If we want our communities to really engage with our vision and mission statements, we must keep them simple. The excellent mission statement of St. Kateri Tekakwitha Parish in Santa Clarita, California, is simple and repeatable: "To hear Jesus' call to be a disciple. To give our lives entirely over to Jesus. To share in Jesus' redemptive mission."

Overcommunicate

A vision or mission statement is not a one-and-done kind of experience. Once you create one, you need to spend time sharing it with the community—and I'm not talking about just putting it in the bulletin. These statements need to be talked about, examined, and explained across various areas of parish life.

In the model of renewal used by Divine Renovation Ministries, Fr. James Mallon recommends having regular vision homilies, in which the pastor uses the readings of the particular Sunday to cast light on the vision and direction of the community. Not only does this remind existing parishioners of the parish's vision and inform new parishioners, but it also helps the community understand why leadership is making particular decisions. These vision homilies invite the members of the congregation to shape their participation in parish life in harmony with the vision and mission.

But parishes shouldn't limit communication of the vision and mission to homilies. Find other creative ways to help your people understand these foundational concepts. Perhaps you can discuss and reflect on them during the first fifteen minutes of every ministry or administrative meeting. Perhaps you can delegate "ambassadors"—women and men who have a deep understanding of the vision and mission—to spend time with the various groups in your parish, answering questions and talking about what these statements mean for the life of the community.

Ideally, all your staff, key leadership (for example, pastoral council members, finance council members, and ministry heads), and most engaged parishioners will understand and share the vision and mission of the parish with others. Whenever I work with a parish, the very first thing I do is ask staff members if the community has a mission statement; and if so, what is it? If I get puzzled looks and no response, that's a sure sign that the mission statement, such as it is, has no real impact on the life of the community.

Evaluate

When I started my professional career, I worked for a company that had no formal review process. I was young and confident and felt that I was delivering results in the position for which

I had been hired. I had good relationships with my coworkers and management.

Years after I started at that company, however, I discovered that I was completely messing up one area of my job. It was so bad that someone else on staff had to literally redo everything that I turned over in that area. I was mortified. If only there had been a regular review process during which my manager evaluated my performance, I would have been able to correct my mistakes and grow in my ability to add value to the company.

The same holds true in terms of living out the vision and mission you've defined for your community. At regular intervals, gather parishioners and leaders together and evaluate how well the parish is doing relative to these statements. This isn't the time to be polite. It's the time to ask hard questions, such as

- How many disciples have we produced this year?
- Have we clearly articulated our values in light of the vision and mission statements?
- Do we hold people accountable when they don't live up to those values, and do we reward and support those who do?
- How well am I, as a pastoral leader or volunteer, aligning my language, actions, and activities with the mission statement? How can I grow in this regard?
- How are specific ministries aligning with the mission statement, and what do we do about them if they are not?

Vision and mission statements should, at their very best, be a kind of guiding star for the life of the parish. For them to function in that way, however, we must be willing to use them to evaluate the life of the community and our leadership decisions. If we invest the necessary time and care in creating them, they will yield great fruit.

PART TWO

THE
FIVE
PARADIGM
SHIFTS

4

From Institutional Faith to Intentional Faith

My daughter currently takes guitar lessons. She's eight years old, and she gives these lessons the attention that you might expect from a second grader. When she does practice, she dutifully plunks away at the various notes with gusto. At this point in her guitar journey, however, she isn't so much playing music as she is moving from note to note with a kind of mechanical ferocity. There is an *interiority* to musicianship that goes beyond strumming the chords—and my daughter has yet to experience this. Right now she is focused on the externals of guitar playing—the chords, timing, and rests that make up songs.

The move from externals to internals is exactly what a shift from a paradigm of *institutional* faith to a paradigm of *intentional* faith requires.

To be clear, when we talk about a paradigm of institutional faith, we're not making the case that the institution of the Church is bad. This is not a statement of ecclesiology but rather an observation on the personal experience of many Catholics within a parish or diocesan cultural context.

Institutional Faith

God has created us to be in an intimate, personal relationship with him; he has given us his very life. Certainly we experience the love of God as a people, and that love is mediated to us through the Church. But, on a personal level, many Catholics experience God as distant and disconnected from the everyday realities of their life, a kind of pious or moral abstraction. When this becomes the normal experience for a large number of Catholics, that standard is replicated and becomes the expectation. In this institutional paradigm, Catholics primarily relate to God through institutional activities, such as going to Mass or taking part in devotions like the Rosary and the Chaplet of Divine Mercy. They may have little understanding that their own personal response to God's invitation has anything to do with their spiritual life.

If you ask a Catholic if they have a personal relationship with Jesus, for example, they will often say, "Yes, I go to Mass." Of course, attending Mass and receiving Holy Communion are essential for Catholics, as a means of deepening their relationship with Christ. Yet people go to church for many reasons, and those acting from an institutional paradigm may lack interiority, like my daughter playing the guitar. In such a paradigm, the fulfillment of the obligation or activity becomes the focus as well as the source of merit. This fosters a kind of transactional mentality, in which Catholics do this thing, fulfill this obligation, say this prayer in order to "get" something (like God's approval or the promise of eternal life). I push this button, pull this lever, and out comes my reward.

I have met many Catholics in my travels, for example, who participate in the First Friday Devotion to the Sacred Heart. This devotion began around 1673, when Jesus, appearing to a French Visitation nun, St. Margaret Mary Alacoque, asked the Church to honor his Sacred Heart. He requested that the faithful receive Holy Communion on the first Friday of each month for nine consecutive months, promising that those who did so would be given an opportunity for final repentance at the moment of death and would not die without receiving last rites, if needed.

This is a beautiful and powerful devotion intended to draw us closer to the person of Jesus Christ. It is fundamentally about relationship. Yet in an institutional paradigm, the relational aspects can get lost. In my own circle, for example, I know Catholics who attend First Friday Masses and then, just in case those don't work, do the First Saturday Devotions, an ancient but entirely different devotion, as a sort of backup measure. These devotions become less about relationship and more about fire insurance!

Because of this transactional mentality, many Catholics neither expect nor experience the fruits of relationship with Christ: inner freedom, peace, joy, transformation, a greater sense of purpose, healing, wholeness, justice, and so forth. The idea that the power, presence, and person of Jesus Christ could radically transform our brokenness and ease our burdens isn't even an imaginative option for many. That God wants to break into our lives and radically change us through the power of his love can seem like a dream or an ancient story with no bearing on life today.

In addition, when people see their relationship with God as transactional, they tend to take on the role of a consumer. Think of the language that many of our Catholic brothers and sisters use in relation to parish life: "I want my children to 'get' all their sacraments." "I'm here to 'get' Communion." In some parishes, many Catholics leave Mass right after receiving Jesus—as if the Holy Sacrifice of the Mass were simply a delivery vehicle for Holy Communion, something to be endured until the prize is awarded.

ABLAZE

One difficulty with a consumer mentality is that consumers often become price conscious. In a paradigm of institutional faith, any attempt to deepen sacramental preparation by adding events or increasing parent or child responsibility can be seen as "raising the price" for that sacrament. That may not be the language they use, but these consumers will often find the sacrament at a cheaper price by going to a nearby parish whose process isn't as demanding.

The result is that parish and diocesan staff members in an institutional paradigm are primarily concerned with meeting the expectations of consumers by providing institutional activities at a regular "price." Staff members can give little consideration to fostering or exploring people's relationship with Christ through a specific event or activity. How often, for example, do we prepare young people to receive the Sacrament of First Holy Communion without ever asking them if they want to follow Jesus as a disciple?

Further, many parish and diocesan staff working within an institutional paradigm don't emphasize communal staff prayer, except for a simple prayer before staff meetings. A quick Our Father, for example, a printed poem or written prayer recited together, or a brief spontaneous intercession by a prayer leader checks the prayer requirement box so that the real work of the meeting can start. In a paradigm of institutional faith, staff prayer also becomes transactional, a task that must be completed so that the staff can move on to the real business. Such prayer doesn't typically bring forth enduring fruit.

To a Paradigm of Intentional Faith

A living faith in Jesus Christ cannot be inherited. You may have grown up in an exceptional Catholic family, but faith, in the theological sense, is both a gift and something with which we must cooperate. No amount of marinating in Catholic identity, Catholic family traditions, and even Catholic prayers will automatically transform us into disciples. At Baptism the Lord gives us the virtue of faith, the capacity to believe. If we were baptized as infants, our parents' faith stood in for us, but at some point, as we grow past the age of reason (seven, according to canon law), we must cooperate with that virtue of faith. We must choose to entrust ourselves to Jesus, to become his disciple.

> For more on how to recognize and foster discipleship in your parish, see appendix A, "Six Disciplines of Discipleship."

One of the greatest challenges in shifting from a paradigm of *institutional* faith to a paradigm of *intentional* faith is overcoming the notion that a relationship with Jesus is somehow a complete mystery—that it's intangible and ineffable and therefore not something we can see in others, let alone talk about with them. But in the Gospels, Jesus is clear regarding what discipleship looks like. He says, "Whoever wishes to come after me must deny himself, take up his cross, and follow me" (Matthew 16:24). Jesus uses active language here. If we want to become disciples, we must "deny," "take up," and "follow." There is an intentionality to discipleship, an interior choice, and a disposition that require an act of the will.

Elements of Living a Paradigm of Institutional Faith

- Primary way of relating to God is through institutional things.
- Parishioners focus on the external practices of the Catholic faith.
- Spiritual practice tends toward the transactional.
- Parishioners act like consumers.
- Pastoral leaders do not spend much time together in prayer.

Elements of Living a Paradigm of Intentional Faith

- Personal relationship with Christ is at the center of community life.
- Staff focuses on facilitating and sustaining that relationship with Christ.
- Leadership teams and pastoral leaders seek the will of the Lord together in prayer.
- Parishioners display active cooperation with the power and person of the Holy Spirit.

In *institutional* faith, the primary mode of relating to God is through institutional activity and the exterior practice of the faith, with little regard for personal disposition, apart from avoiding sin. *Intentional* faith prioritizes a deep trust in the promises of Christ, an ongoing disposition to receive the fruits and gifts of God, and a desire to share those fruits with others.

Intentional faith places relationship with Christ, who lives in the midst of his Church, at the center of community life. This living and intimate relationship with Jesus is the context within which rules and obligations are highlighted, encouraged, and discussed. In this paradigm, a pastor might recommend an experience of mortification of the flesh—not eating meat or fasting, for example—specifically because such an experience fosters solidarity with Jesus, who has given everything so that we might be set free. Fasting, then, is not seen as a transaction—I'll do this if you'll answer my prayer—but as a way of drawing closer to Jesus, joining with him in suffering and sacrifice.

When a parish lives out of this intentional paradigm, staff members understand that God wants all people to experience the fruit of a relationship with him (which includes freedom, healing, wholeness, peace, and joy—the hallmarks of the kingdom of God) in the midst of his Church. Therefore the leadership team focuses on structuring and shaping the life of the parish around this reality. Knowing that Jesus calls every parishioner into an intimate relationship with him, the staff understands that at least part of their role is to foster that relationship. Everything else—including strategy, structure, and staff—revolves around this one central understanding. The burning questions on the hearts of staff and pastoral leaders of a parish rooted in a paradigm of intentional faith are "Where are our people in their lived relationship with God?" and "What can we do to help them grow in that relationship?"

There is another critical element of the paradigm shift to intentional faith: communal prayer. Leadership teams trust that God has given his people supernatural power and authority in the Holy Spirit. He will manifest this power through ordinary men and women who, in partnership with him, do extraordinary things for the kingdom of God. As a result, leadership teams expect, plan for, and leave room for the presence, power, and purpose of the Holy Spirit to accompany their activities. Furthermore, these pastoral leadership teams eagerly seek the will of the Lord together, engaging in frequent prayer—including Eucharistic adoration, Mass, communal intercession, and praying with one another.

Finally, in a paradigm of intentional faith, staff and pastoral leaders are willing to discuss their own relationship with God and share the ups and downs of their spiritual journey with each other and with other parishioners. This kind of vulnerability can inspire others on the leadership team who have never openly shared their personal faith life with others.

5

From Engagement to Encouter

In the wake of the devastating demographic and religious-practice information coming out of places like the Pew Research Center and Gallup, churches have been scrambling to stem the tide of falling membership and aging congregations. Companies and organizations have poured resources into the creation of studies, programs, and processes intended to revitalize church life. A mini-industry has sprung up as churches throw money at one program or another in search of an answer.

Some of the research is very useful. Gallup has published *Growing an Engaged Church*, by Albert Winseman, along with related material, Living Your Strengths and Strengths-Finder 2.0. Many Catholic parishes and a few dioceses have embraced this engagement approach to good effect.

For Winseman, an engaged church is one where people experience spiritual growth, serve others, and share their financial and material abundance. This concept of engagement, in its broadest sense, is about connection. "Engagement," Winseman writes, "is how you feel about your church. . . . [It's] about emotions. Good soil churches have a climate that fosters a deep and strong emotional connection."[15]

Fr. James Mallon and his team have used Gallup's engagement tools in their renewal of Saint Benedict Parish and in their work with Divine Renovation Ministries. Fr. Mallon defines engagement as "a sense of belonging, a psychological connection to the local church and its mission, and a sense of ownership of what is happening and of where the Church is headed."[16] Behind this understanding of engagement is an operational worldview that affirms that *belonging* leads to *believing*, which leads to *behaving*. In his written work, Fr. James makes a compelling case that this model (*belonging believing behaving*) needs to supplant the model present in so many of our parishes, whereby we operate as if *behaving* leads to *believing*, which fosters *belonging*.

I wholeheartedly agree with Fr. James. I also think, as he does, that it is essential to place this model—and this broad understanding of engagement—in the proper context. *Belonging* only leads to *believing* when Christ is the explicit center of community life and when relationship with him is talked about and normalized. One of the reasons that the Divine Renovation approach to parish renewal bears fruit is precisely that they place Jesus at the heart of everything they do. Without this Jesus-centric approach, parishes can easily reduce Gallup's rich understanding of engagement to mere involvement or activity. This is precisely what happens in a paradigm of engagement.

The Engagement Trap

Leaders working from a paradigm of engagement see their primary responsibility as getting people involved in the life of the community—which usually means making sure people are present at parish events, supporting activities, and volunteering. Obviously, these things are desirable, but in a paradigm of engagement, they become the entire focus of leadership's time and energy. In this view of parish life, the highest goods are involvement, volunteering, and activity. These become ends in themselves, and often they are not integrally connected to developing a relationship with Jesus or to mission.

Seen from this perspective, action and activity become confused with vitality. Leaders, key volunteers, and involved parishioners evaluate the life of the community based on its level of activity. In my years of ministry and exposure to hundreds of parishes, I have heard numerous leaders say that their parish is "so alive because of all the ministries and activities that we have available"—as if motion were synonymous with mission.

The human body—with its complex chemical, biological, and mechanical processes—offers some parallels in this regard. Your heart, for example, pumps blood through a network of interconnected arteries, veins, and capillaries. This cardiovascular highway has a very particular purpose: it brings oxygen to the organs and muscles of the body and removes waste, such as carbon dioxide. The arteries carry blood away from your heart, and veins carry blood toward your heart. If the arteries and veins simply decided to do whatever—if there was no rhyme or reason to the direction that blood flowed—your organs would die from oxygen starvation.

In short, biological activity without a particular purpose leads to death. The same is true of a parish. Parishes with lots of activities, ministries, and socializing opportunities are not necessarily vital, alive, or transformed. They may simply be busy.

ABLAZE

The mission of the Church, however, is to make disciples. Therefore, if we want to gauge the vitality and life of our parishes, the real question we should be asking is not "How many ministries or activities do we have available?" but rather "How many disciples have we produced?" Jesus called the Church into being to bear the fruit of discipleship. It doesn't matter how active it is if it is not producing that fruit.

Consider the case of the barren fig tree in chapter 13 of the Gospel of Luke. This tree is alive, and yet it has not produced fruit for the vineyard owner. On some level, this tree is active: sap and nutrients move between its roots and its branches. And yet it does not bear fruit. In a similar way, some parishes I have encountered are exceptionally active and yet spiritually dead.

The question of fruit bearing is the single most important question we can ask ourselves as parishes. Yet communities in a paradigm of engagement often don't have the time or the framework to even consider the question. Because action, volunteerism, and participation are the prime goods of these parishes, leadership teams often skip discernment processes. Instead they tend to "throw bodies" at problems, opportunities, or gaps in the organizational structure.

For example, discernment for service in a particular ministry in many parishes boils down to this: a parish needs a lector, a catechist, an Extraordinary Minister of Holy Communion, or someone to bring Communion to the sick, so they send out a call and then take whoever shows up. In a paradigm of engagement, availability is the major criterion we use to determine whether someone should be part of a particular ministry.

When we operate out of this value, we unwittingly do a disservice to the uniqueness of our brothers and sisters in Christ. What we are unintentionally saying is "Your unique combination of natural talents, strengths, spiritual gifts, and experience don't matter. I just need a body. Anyone will do." As a result, we don't bear fruit, because we are not aligning areas of service with the spiritual gifts, talents, and strengths of individuals.

In addition, placing someone in an area of ministry for which they might not be spiritually or naturally gifted is a recipe for trouble. If your parish frequently has to replace individuals in ministry because they abruptly leave or "flame out," your parish might be caught in a paradigm of engagement.

A Paradigm of Encounter

The word "encounter" has a rich history. It originated from two Latin words, *in* and *contra* (literally "in against"). As the word developed, especially in Middle English usage, it took on an even more martial meaning: a clash of adversaries. Encounters, therefore, are relational experiences where something important is at stake, where there is the potential for change.

Encounters matter—and in terms of connecting with another person, an encounter differs from a meeting. I see this played out in my daily life. I meet many people in my ministry; I get to know names and faces, and I feel blessed to be even a small part of their story. However, every so often I have an encounter with an individual, a heart-to-heart experience that leaves me deeply changed. There is a clear difference between meeting someone and encountering someone. This is especially true in

Catholic parish life, where many of our people meet Jesus in the Mass but very few seem to encounter him.

The paradigm of encounter addresses this fundamental issue. Leaders who have made the journey into a paradigm of encounter see, discern, and evaluate every facet of community life from this one essential perspective: how well does each area of parish life foster, nourish, and support an encounter with the Father, in Jesus Christ, through the power of the Holy Spirit? Over time these leaders develop strategic pathways in the community that can lead people from encounter to encounter, all the while providing opportunities to support individuals as their encounters lead to discipleship and into missionary discipleship. (See chapter 7, "From Programs to People," for more information on this.)

A parish rooted in an encounter paradigm would, of course, ask how Eucharistic Adoration fosters an encounter with Jesus for parishioners. But that parish wouldn't stop there. It would also ask, "How does our current parish registration process nurture or sustain an encounter with Jesus Christ?" The truth is, it absolutely should. And yet, when I ask that question of parish teams that come to conferences, the response is almost always silence, puzzled looks, and a few gasps as they start to get it. Often we are so rooted in our current paradigms that it never occurs to us to ask a question like this. Yet our parish registration process can open the door to profound encounters with Jesus if we approach it with that in mind.

My friend John (not his real name) is the director of evangelization in a diocese in the United States. One day he went undercover and visited three Protestant megachurches in his area. In each case, he posed as a Catholic who drove by the church regularly and spent some time on its website. He said that he was interested in what the church was about and wanted to know how he could join. This was a fascinating experiment, but even more fascinating was the response John received at these churches.

In each community, someone came out to speak with him, and the conversation lasted at least forty-five minutes. These folks didn't spend a lot of time talking with him about their church but rather asking John questions about his own life, specifically what he was looking for in life, faith, and church. And then they listened to him. At the end of these conversations, each of them let John know the ways their community could walk with him on his journey.

John confided to me that the difference between the Catholic approach to registration and the approach he experienced at these non-Catholic communities was striking. The process for registering at a Catholic parish is often impersonal. "Fill out this form, email it, or hand it in at the office, and you'll start receiving envelopes in three to four weeks." At best we might spend time talking with potential new parishioners about all the ways they can get involved—which is a polite and subtle way of saying, "Here are all of the things you can do for us." In contrast, John was quite moved by his experiences at the Protestant communities. In his conversations there, he felt the love of Jesus flowing to him. It was clear that, like Jesus, these evangelical leaders cared about him and wanted to invest their life in him. The power of such encounters should never be underestimated.

ABLAZE

In order for parishes to live out an encounter paradigm, staff, leaders, and key volunteers must be willing to take an honest look at the activities of their church community. Then they must be willing to "own" when a particular ministry, process, or event is not actually fostering an encounter with Jesus—even if that activity is popular, well respected, or historically important to the parish. The good news is that typically you won't need to completely eliminate activities that fail to foster encounter (although you might need to do that in order to focus your efforts on renewal and concentrate your limited resources). Rather, a few simple tweaks to an event or process usually can connect that activity more directly with your parish's mission and help lead participants into an encounter with Jesus Christ.

I know a parish catechetical leader who is responsible for Confirmation preparation. Her annual meeting with parents of the students amounted to a dry recitation of the administrative rules around the sacramental program. I worked with her to help her understand the spiritual journey that people make toward Jesus. In response, she made a few changes to the program, leaving space for the parents to hear and absorb the basic gospel message. Those simple changes had a profound effect on parents and catechists alike. A hunger began to arise in that community—a desire for intimacy with Jesus. The full effects of that tweaking are yet to be determined.

It's never too late to foster encounter!

Finally, leaders in a paradigm of encounter take the time to get to know people, their gifts, and where they might be on their spiritual journey, before thrusting them into service.

These leaders believe that connecting areas of giftedness with particular areas of service will yield the greatest fruit. To that end, they support and create discernment processes designed to match people's gifts with service opportunities.

Elements of Living in a Paradigm of Engagement

- Leadership is focused almost entirely on activity and involvement.
- Discernment processes are skipped in searches for volunteers.
- Availability is valued over specific giftedness or experience.
- Motion is equated with mission and vitality.
- Tendency is to convert people to the community rather than to Christ.

Elements of Living in a Paradigm of Encounter

- Community sees and evaluates its life through the lens of encounter with Jesus.
- Community intentionally modifies and creates events so that they foster encounters with Jesus.
- Discernment processes connect giftedness with areas of service.

I know of a parish where the leaders of the music ministry developed a comprehensive process for discerning whether to accept potential members. Here's how it goes: during meeting number one, the prospective member hears about the ministry from the leaders, who describe the purpose and nature of their ministry as service to the worshipping community and to the outside world. After that discussion, the music ministry leaders pray with the prospective member and ask the person to continue to pray about serving in the ministry. Two weeks later, the music ministry leaders and the prospective member come together again to share the fruit of their prayer. If both sides feel there is a call from God to pursue music ministry, they arrange for the prospective member to sit in on the next rehearsal.

This third meeting (the rehearsal) allows the music ministry team to gauge the person's natural talents and spiritual gifts. It also allows everyone involved to get a feel for whether the person would mesh well with the group. Assuming that things still seem positive, the leaders extend a formal invitation to join the music ministry. The new member must agree to attend regular practices and learn the music before singing or playing with the ministry on a full-time basis.

That process may seem like overkill, but this music ministry is filled with disciples who possess a great array of spiritual gifts and natural talents. The musicians report that the discernment process itself fosters an encounter with Christ. For their part, the music leadership team, by faithfully listening for the movement of the Holy Spirit and avoiding the standard volunteer sign-up approach, has formed a group that fosters powerful encounters with Jesus through their music. The fruitfulness of this ministry cannot be denied. People report a deeper level of participation in the Mass when this group leads the music; the ministry has also played for parishioners who are gravely ill and in the process of dying.

Imagine what could happen if we took this level of discernment and this focus on encounter as seriously in every area of parish life.

It is important to note here that the various paradigm shifts interlink to support and strengthen each other, while maintaining their own integrity. Consider the paradigms of encounter and intentional faith, for example. The paradigm of encounter looks at how facets of parish life foster discrete, particular encounters with God, and the paradigm of intentional faith sees how those encounters can fit into a larger journey toward a personal and intentional faith in Jesus Christ in the midst of his Church.

6

From Maintenance to Mission

I have a problem with stewardship.

Not with the Church's understanding of stewardship or the theology behind it. My issue has to do with the imagery we use when communicating about stewardship and how parish culture often distorts that imagery. In the parable of the talents (Matthew 25:14-30), it is clear that the good steward—the one who embodies the principles of the kingdom of God—is the servant who risked the most, who traded and invested the wealth he had received from his master. The kingdom principle here is that the one who releases what he has and pours it out in good measure for others will receive even more—because the kingdom of God is about abundance, generation, multiplication, and new life. This isn't primarily a strategy of wealth management but a demand of love, which is why Jesus says that "whoever wishes to save his life will lose it, but whoever loses his life for my sake will find it" (Matthew 16:25). When we break open our life for the sake of others, we are living in the heart of the Father's love, which always seeks the beloved.

And yet, in a time of declining attendance, shrinking resources, and fewer volunteers, stewardship at the parish level often becomes about conservation. The image of the steward is reduced to that of a conservationist—a person who gives of their time, talent, and treasure so that the community can continue to exist. In this context, stewardship isn't about investing for mission; it's about laying in stores for a long, hard winter. In his phenomenal book *Doing the Math of Mission*, Gil Rendle teases out a fascinating distinction between counting and measuring that bears directly on what I have tried to describe above:

> *Counting is giving attention to numbers.* When counting, the question to be answered is "How many?" Conversations about "How many?" are most frequently conversations about resources. Conversations about resources, in a time of limited resources, are commonly conversations about scarcity—"Do we have enough?" or "How can we get more?"
>
> *Measuring is giving attention to change.* When measuring, the question is not "How many?" but rather "How far?" Conversations about "How far?" are frequently about change that can be measured over time, as in "How far have we come, over the past year, toward our goal?"[17]

In our current season of limited resources, our parishes focus heavily on counting, which directs our time and energy toward issues of scarcity, and which in turn causes us to value maintenance. In many ways, our response has become that of the bad steward in Jesus' parable, who buried the wealth his master gave him because he was afraid. This burying of wealth translates into an almost entirely inward focus on the survival of the community and a "missionary amnesia"—an almost total forgetting of the Church's primary mission to make disciples.

Cardinal Jorge Mario Bergoglio addressed the College of Cardinals during their general congregation before the conclave that would elect him pope. He identified this inward focus as a major issue in the life of the Church:

> When the Church does not go out of herself to evangelize, she becomes self-referential; she grows ill (like the stooped woman in the Gospel). The evils which appear throughout history in Church institutions are rooted in this self-referentiality—a kind of theological narcissism.[18]

Unfortunately, the pope's comments ring true: too many parishes and dioceses throughout the world are ill. We have become self-referential, have turned inward, and are concerned primarily with our own survival. This is the essential experience of living in a paradigm of maintenance.

Stuck in the Maintenance Shop

Parishes rooted in a paradigm of maintenance possess an inward vision. The community's survival is the primary driver of budgets, allocations of resources, and activity. Staff members, leaders, and key volunteers in maintenance-focused parishes spend an inordinate amount of their time keeping the trains running on time—that is, finding volunteers, maintaining processes and programs, and keeping structures alive. The primary value for leaders in this paradigm is getting—and keeping—people in the pews.

There's nothing wrong with making sure the inner life of a community continues in a positive direction, and there's nothing wrong with fostering volunteers and raising up men and women who coordinate the actions and activities of parish life. In fact, if we want to fruitfully live out our mission, it is essential that we have solid structures and processes in place that can maintain the health and vitality of our parishes.

In a paradigm of maintenance, however, mission is rarely considered, and maintenance is seen as an end in itself. We may care for those who make their way to our doors, and we may even have some outreach activities, but these are often seen as "good" things to do and are not connected to a fundamental sense of mission or purpose for the community. And so we invest the majority of our time and money in activities that support the interior life of the community. We reject spending funds for other things not seen as essential—things like initiatives that take place outside the confines of our parish buildings.

Just look at the disparity between what parishes typically spend on the religious education of children, for example, relative to what they might spend on an evangelizing outreach, a hunger initiative, or a social justice effort. Whatever we might state as a written value in parish websites, bulletins, and strategic plans, such a discrepancy between interior activity and missionary outreach is an example of a *lived value*. We invest in what we believe in—and in a maintenance paradigm, our beliefs center around the protection, survival, and well-being of our parish. This is our primary concern.

To be clear, parishioners and leaders who support a maintenance approach aren't acting maliciously. In fact, many are motivated by love of the community. Christian writer William Sloane Coffin explains it this way:

Most church boats don't like to be rocked; they prefer to lie at anchor rather than go places in stormy seas. But that's because we Christians view the Church as the object of our love instead of the subject and instrument of God's.[19]

The danger in a paradigm of maintenance is that our love for the Church, and in particular the survival of our own parish, can obscure a sense of mission. We tend to forget that the parish doesn't primarily exist for us but is rather an instrument of the love and mercy of God to be sent out into the world.

In a maintenance paradigm, our love for the parish can become possessive: we can confuse membership with ownership. When that happens, we start to talk about "my" parish, as in "How dare they try to change my parish!" and "This is how we do things here, in my parish." A personal stake in our parish communities is a good thing, but the reality is that parishes don't exist primarily for our edification or as nodes in our social networks. They also are not simply sociological groupings that help define our identity. In fact, parishes are *missionary outposts* of the diocese called to bring the light of Christ into the local civic community and the lives of those within the boundaries of the parish.

Rather than being missionary communities ready to welcome newcomers with gratitude, parishes rooted in a paradigm of maintenance can become closed off and insular. One pastor I worked for recounted a story from when he was a seminarian interning at a local parish. That parish sat in a rapidly developing area, so he took flyers and parish information and dropped them off at the new homes and planned communities that were springing up. Once, as he was grabbing flyers from the office, the parish secretary accosted him and demanded to know what he was doing. When he explained, the secretary shot him a hard look. "Stop doing that," she shouted. "We have enough people coming here to this parish, and we don't want any more!"

Whether this sentiment is stated publicly or just reinforced quietly through a lack of missionary activity or the way we treat people when they come to the parish, it is present in too many of our communities.

In a maintenance-oriented parish, mission-focused proposals are sometimes seen as potential threats to the well-being of the community. Often this is related to an emphasis on counting, resources, and scarcity. Continuing his discussion of metrics and mission, Gil Rendle says:

> Conversations about resources/inputs (dollars, time, buildings) and activities/throughputs (programs, groups, projects) easily become worrisome and anxiety-producing conversations about what we have, what we need and how to get more. These are conversations heavily marked by problem solving and either caring for, or fixing, the church we love.[20]

Often the solution people see to these problems is to reject any investments in mission.

Some years ago, I was engaged in a brainstorming session on evangelization led by my pastor and including parish staff members (of which I was one) and parish council members. My pastor asked everyone to throw out some ideas for evangelization. As might be expected in a parish dominated by a maintenance orientation, almost all the suggestions focused on reaching out to those people who would come to pretty much anything we did, such as a Bible study, or on events that would take place within the walls of the community, including having better coffee and donuts after Mass! The result was that only those comfortable in the parish or already members would experience whatever evangelistic outreach we came up with.

Our parish sat right next to a water park owned by the park district in our village. This park didn't have enough parking available for its patrons, and our parish had acres of parking. During the summer, we allowed visitors to the water park to park in our lot and walk over to the attraction.

When it was my turn to share some evangelization ideas, I rather innocently suggested that perhaps we could set up a booth at the edge of our parking lot. As individuals walked by our booth to get to the water park, we could introduce ourselves and offer a goody bag with a couple of water bottles and some sunscreen. As we engaged these people in conversation, we could ask them if they would like prayer for anything and give them our best wishes for a great day at the water park.

As I looked around the room, I was stunned by the looks on my colleagues' faces. You would have thought that I had suggested launching a manned mission to Mars! The resistance was almost immediate. Again and again, the major issue people brought up was the cost and liability of such an outreach. The very same objections were raised when I suggested that our parish rent an inflatable movie screen and invite the local neighborhood once a month during the summer to watch a family movie in our oversized parking lot. We could provide popcorn and give families a safe place to picnic as they watched a film together. In their objections, the leadership of that parish sent a message: we cannot let a nonessential initiative—missionary outreach—threaten that which is essential: the stability and financial viability of the community.

Now, am I saying that financial viability is unimportant or that we shouldn't be good stewards of the resources we do have? Of course not.

But prudential judgment on balancing a parish's budget can mask fear. And remember the kingdom principle: the one who invests and gives away receives! The good steward was the one who risked. In a paradigm of maintenance, however, there is little tolerance for risk; therefore our parishes, because they focus almost exclusively on their own survival, cannot receive the riches that the Lord wants to pour out in good measure

In terms of budgeting, leaders in maintenance-focused parishes concern themselves with numbers. In other words, they value throughput: How many people did we put through our programs, processes, and events? How many people attended Bible study? How many Baptisms have we had? How many weddings and funerals? What is our October count for Mass attendance? These numbers become a standard for measuring success and vitality.

As in the engagement paradigm, this kind of obsession with throughput confuses motion with mission and activity with fruit. Remember that *counting* concerns itself primarily with numbers, and *measuring* concerns itself primarily with change or outcomes. Counting is a value of a maintenance paradigm. If we want to arrive at a way to capture real vitality, growth, and renewal in our parishes, we have to break out of the maintenance trap and embrace a paradigm of mission.

Embracing the Mindset of Mission

Staff, pastoral leaders, and key volunteers who embrace a paradigm of mission approach the life, identity, and activity of the parish and parishioners in radically different ways than do those who lead out of a maintenance paradigm. Leaders in a mission-focused parish understand that the parish exists in the world for the sake of the world. Their primary concern is not with keeping people in the pews but with releasing the power of the gospel in the world outside the Catholic community. Therefore they spend the bulk of their energy on creating structures and processes that raise up and equip ordinary men and women to share the love of the Father in Jesus Christ with others; fostering opportunities for the parish to reach out to the local community; and organizing the infrastructure of the parish community to support a robust vision of missionary activity.

In his encyclical *The Joy of the Gospel*, Pope Francis puts forth a call for precisely this kind of missionary mindset:

> I dream of a "missionary option," that is, a missionary impulse capable of transforming everything, so that the Church's customs, ways of doing things, times and schedules, language and structures can be suitably channeled for the evangelization of today's world rather than for her self-preservation. The renewal of structures demanded by pastoral conversion can only be understood in this light: as part of an effort to make them more mission minded.[21]

ABLAZE

Francis understands that the Church and her parishes must be grounded in mission and must view every other facet of life through that lens. In other words, mission should drive structure, strategy, budgeting, hiring, and so on. This is precisely the mindset of those engaged in a paradigm of mission. Leadership teams who embrace a missionary paradigm are willing to make sometimes difficult decisions and redesign structures, processes, and activities so that they more fruitfully support mission. Missionary criteria are the standard by which they discern, choose, form, and evaluate pastoral leaders. That's a challenge for many parishes, because most of our current leadership has been chosen and evaluated according to maintenance criteria. The missionary mindset does not come naturally to them.

Leaders in mission-focused parishes also understand that the primary responsibility for the transformation of the local civic community—and by extension, the world—lies with the lay men and women of the parish, not the ordained or the full-time staff. In other words, Christ calls every baptized person not only into a personal relationship but also into a missionary lifestyle. This orientation allows the baptized to be an effective channel of God's transformative love for the world in a way consistent with their vocation and state in life.

When we operate from a paradigm of maintenance, however, and constantly focus on the need for resources and the desire to keep people in the pews, we tend to see our parishioners through the lens of their wounds, not their primary identity as sons and daughters of the Most High God. Because of that, we don't expect much for them or from them. We consider it quite normal when they not only lack personal transformation but also don't have an impact on the transformation of the world.

In a paradigm of mission, on the other hand, staff, leaders, and key volunteers do not view parishioners primarily as people with particular wounds and needs. Rather they see parishioners as competent men and women, gifted by God and called by him to release the power of the kingdom into the world. Nowhere have I found this radical missionary identity and expectation described better than by Banning Liebscher in his book *Jesus Culture*:

> You and I are part of a revolution. We are appointed to overthrow the government of darkness that has enslaved people in sin and sickness and to establish the Kingdom of Light on earth as it is in Heaven. Our revolution is not a worldly anarchy of violence and control; it is a heavenly reformation of *truth*—spoken and demonstrated in love and the supernatural power of God. You were never created to hide, cowering in some corner, subordinate to evil. Rather, you were born to step out into the midst of darkness—to confront fear, nullify destruction and pain, and rebuild with life and hope.
>
> . . . Jesus freely and unrestrainedly grants us the authority He has been given on the earth. We are delegated to shape culture with Heaven's perspective and purpose, to serve with peaceful strength and dignity, to deliberate compassionately, and to operate with kindness.[22]

ABLAZE

This is who we are, and this is why the Lord gathers us together, so that we can be sent into the world as salt, light, and leaven—impacting hearts, cities, cultures, countries, and civilizations with the power of the gospel.

Pope John Paul II, in reflecting on the identity of lay men and women, put it this way:

> Because the lay faithful belong to Christ, Lord and King of the Universe, they share in his kingly mission and are called by him to spread that Kingdom in history. They exercise their kingship as Christians, above all in the spiritual combat in which they seek to overcome in themselves the kingdom of sin (cf. Romans 6:12), and then to make a gift of themselves so as to serve, in justice and in charity, Jesus who is himself present in all his brothers and sisters, above all in the very least (cf. Matthew 25:40).

> But in particular the lay faithful are called to restore to creation all its original value. In ordering creation to the authentic well-being of humanity in an activity governed by the life of grace, they share in the exercise of the power with which the Risen Christ draws all things to himself and subjects them along with himself to the Father, so that God might be everything to everyone (cf. 1 Corinthians 15:28; John 12:32).[23]

Parishes living out of a paradigm of mission embrace this understanding and nurture this identity of their members while adopting a radical orientation outward, toward the world. Leadership discernment and formation, as well as programs and processes, are all influenced by this missionary focus.

Not surprisingly, leaders in a mission-focused paradigm value *measuring* more than *counting*. Rather than being fixated on numbers, resources, and attendance, they focus on outcomes. In other words, they evaluate programs and processes not on how many people go through them but on the impact they have relative to relationship with Jesus and the transformation of the world according to kingdom principles. It's not that numbers, attendance, and budgets are unimportant, but leaders in a paradigm of mission don't mistake these things for vitality and fruit.

Where Are We?

Many Catholic parishes are rooted in maintenance; missionary-focused communities are quite rare. When I speak to parishes on this topic, staff and leaders often ask me how you can tell if you have moved into a paradigm of mission. This book provides a Cultural Snapshot Inventory (see appendix C) that will help make that determination, but I usually tell leaders that they can ask themselves two questions to get a sense of where their particular community might be:

1. What percentage of your parish budget is devoted to things that are primarily focused inside the community versus primarily oriented to the local civic community or other outreach?

2. What are the three biggest issues facing the civic community in which your parish is placed, and what is your parish doing specifically to address those needs?

Elements of Living in a Paradigm of Maintenance

- Vision, action, and activity of the parish are focused inward.
- The majority of the time, energy, and resources of the parish are geared toward "keeping the trains running on time."
- There is a strong emphasis on throughput (attendance, numbers, and resources).
- Leadership tends to see parishioners primarily as wounded and in need.

Elements of Living in a Paradigm of Mission

- The vision, action, and activity of the parish are focused outward.
- The time, energy, and resources of the parish are geared toward the transformation of the local community and the world through the power of the gospel.
- Attention is on fruitfulness, transformation, and change rather than attendance and numbers.
- Parishioners are seen as empowered sons and daughters sent into the world for its renewal and transformation.

The point of these questions, and really of any tool used to find out where a parish might be culturally, is not to make the leaders in that parish feel bad but to reveal a starting point for renewal efforts. Transitioning to a paradigm of mission is possible without having a fully formed missionary approach to the world. If your staff, leaders, and key volunteers can make this shift and start approaching the life of the community from this perspective, the vision and life of your parish will begin to change in radical ways.

7

From Programs to People

I remember the first time a parish paid me to be their Confirmation coordinator.

The pastor of that parish reached out to me because I had done a lot of volunteer work with their high school youth ministry program. They were in a bind and needed someone to step up immediately. I said yes and quickly set to work creating a pathway for those preparing for Confirmation to encounter Jesus and start living as disciples. I focused entirely on the spiritual development and fruitfulness of those teens, and my excitement grew at the prospect of taking this journey with them.

Imagine my surprise when I started to receive pushback from the pastor and some of the staff. My new approach was causing havoc not only with the processes surrounding sacramental preparation but also with the established way that the parish did ministry. My focus was on the spiritual growth of the teens. I failed to understand that this pastor had hired me primarily to run an established program smoothly. He wanted the trains to run on time; he didn't want the established tracks demolished and new ones built.

Of course, spiritual growth and program excellence are not mutually exclusive. But let's face it, the Catholic Church is huge, and we have become adept at creating programs and processes that move large numbers of people from one place to another, especially in our Catholic school systems, sacramental preparation programs, and catechetical offerings. This is especially true of the Church in North America, which largely grew from the influx of immigrants coming to the continent. To handle the flow of our people, we built physical and organizational structures, processes, and programs that focused on producing fully initiated Catholics who could integrate with the surrounding secular culture.

We've inherited that program mentality, and often our first instinct when faced with things like declining attendance, fewer resources, and lack of participation is to "tune up" our programs and find ways to increase their efficiency. It reminds me of a video I once watched in which the speaker made a comparison between the Church and a shoe factory. The purpose of a shoe factory, he said, was to produce shoes. If the factory wasn't producing shoes, then it didn't matter whether that factory had the best equipment, the most well-trained employees, or the highest quality raw materials—there was a problem in the factory. Similarly, the speaker continued, the purpose of the Church is to make disciples, and if the Church isn't making disciples, then it doesn't matter if we have the "fulness of truth" and all seven sacraments, or that through our bishops we can pass on the revelation of God in Jesus Christ with complete integrity and lack of error. There is a problem in the Church. This problem isn't one of ontology—of the nature of the Church herself. Rather the issue is in the way that we are living out our common baptismal vocation as a people.

I often take this shoe factory analogy and extend it when I speak at conferences or consult with individual parishes. If my company had a shoe factory that wasn't producing shoes, I would bring in someone to turn that factory around. However, that individual would most likely have to have a deep understanding of the shoe-making process from beginning to end or have to bring in someone with that experience. Without that firsthand experience, it would be difficult to analyze the workflow on the factory floor and create a machine and line layout that would maximize the efficiency of the shoe-making process. It would also be difficult to set up standards for quality control and employee evaluation.

The same holds true for the renewal of our parishes. The disciple-making process cannot be understood from the outside or from a place of theory. Unless parish leaders have experience helping others encounter Jesus, walking with them into discipleship, maturing them as disciples, and equipping them to share Jesus with others, it will be difficult for them to embrace the values and take the actions necessary to transform a parish culture.

This is one of the most significant issues facing us today—as significant as the overall lack of disciples in our communities. We have leaders who are responsible for the evangelization of hundreds, thousands, tens of thousands, and even hundreds of thousands but who have never evangelized a single person. And it shows.

Without this kind of experience, our leaders default to an overly programmatic approach that overlooks the individual spiritual journeys of our people. Sherry Weddell, in her book *Fruitful Discipleship*, explains it this way:

> I once heard a shrewd Dominican pastor observe that because of our numbers, American pastors and parish leaders tend to do religion "wholesale, not retail." We move hundreds through the sacramental prep and various catechetical and service programs,

while telling ourselves that we do not have the luxury of attending to God's grace at work in individuals.[24]

As we have shown, this isn't simply a function of numbers but also a byproduct of limited evangelizing experience among our leaders. Add to this the influence of the paradigms of institutional faith, engagement, and maintenance, and you have a perfect storm for the creation of another paradigm focused on a programmatic approach to parish renewal.

Get with the Program

Parishes and dioceses living out of a paradigm of programs tend to value operational expertise and administrative skill, often seeing them as the primary or essential skill set in ministry. Administrative excellence is critical to the flourishing of a parish or diocese; but in a programmatic paradigm, it seldom occurs to the hiring manager or pastor to ask candidates questions about their own lived relationship with Jesus or their practical experience of leading someone into discipleship. Furthermore, in this program paradigm, employees, staff, and volunteers are often evaluated—praised or criticized, rewarded or punished—primarily on their execution of operational tasks and their ability to handle administrative loads.

Remember that pastor who asked me to handle Confirmation? At the end of that year, he evaluated my performance as poor, despite the fact that a large number of those confirmed became disciples of Jesus Christ and matured as disciples while attending our youth ministry program over the next three years. Were there things that I could have done better in terms of operations and execution? Absolutely! However, the pastor rated my work only against the standard of administration. The spiritual fruit never entered into the equation.

It's usually at this point in my presentation of this paradigm shift that someone in my audience says something like "But I'm the DRE, and I don't spend much one-on-one time with the children in my program, so why make such a big deal of experience (or lack thereof) in evangelizing someone?" After shooting up a quick prayer for the gift of diplomacy, I usually affirm what they pointed out—that in their role they don't spend much time with the children—but then I challenge them. They may not spend time with the children, but they spend time with the catechists who spend time with the children. The evangelizing context of their ministry may not be children but the adults who minister to those children.

The truth is that *textbooks don't make disciples, events don't make disciples, and programs don't make disciples. People make disciples.* And DREs have direct contact with those individuals who can lead children into relationship with Jesus. But if you are not a disciple yourself, with some practical experience discipling others, how can you discern where catechists are on their spiritual journey, whether they are called by God to be catechists, and whether they are able to evangelize children? How can you provide good evangelizing curricula and raise up a generation of missionary catechists?

Leaders in a paradigm of programs often hold to the belief that programs do, in fact, make disciples. Consequently they see the right program as the primary solution to a problem or as the driver of renewal. In chapter 2, we discussed why there is no such thing as a programmatic silver bullet, but this lack of a cure-all is a source of frustration, anxiety, and burnout for many parish leaders. They seek after the holy grail of programs, get excited about the one they think will make the difference, and then deal with disappointment when that program or event doesn't have the desired effect.

Another feature of a program-focused paradigm is a non-specific, meandering cycle of programs and events. Leaders offer programs based on perceived needs, personal interest, or a sense that they are obliged to offer something—anything—for their people. They present these programs and events as faith enrichment or adult education, discrete experiences that are not integrated into a larger journey of formation. In other words, leaders move people from program to program *without specifically understanding how these programs could build on one another to form mission-minded disciples.*

A parish influenced by this paradigm, for example, might offer *The Great Adventure Bible Study* series in the fall, then use the *Oremus* video study of prayer in the spring, then switch to Word on Fire's *Catholicism* product in the summer, returning to the Bible during the following fall with a *Great Adventure* study of the Psalms. Each of these programs contains excellent, high-quality, high-impact content delivered in a professional and consumer-friendly manner. But unless church leaders connect these programs to each other in a way that creates a pathway to discipleship, maturity, and missionary identity, they and their people miss out on any synergistic effect these programs could have.

This is a critical drawback for programmatic paradigms: a lack of vision for parish renewal and diocesan transformation.

As Sherry Weddell writes:

> Without an absolute, non-negotiable, vision of the human fruit
> we are supposed to bear, we cannot discern what kinds of pas-
> toral structures we really need. We will not be able to recognize
> where we are failing, and we won't be able to identify obstacles.
> We cannot revise our pastoral practices to foster more abundant
> fruit-bearing unless our purpose is clear from the beginning.[25]

This lack of vision makes it difficult for leaders to imagine
what a discipleship pathway might look like, because they have
no clear idea about what the end result looks like.

Further, leaders operating from a program-focused paradigm
don't usually do personal follow-up after a program or event.
They tend not to ask about the effect, or fruit, of a program in
the lives of attendees, preferring once again to talk about the
success of the program in terms of numbers.

In my own parish, Queen of the Rosary near Chicago, we
used Ascension Press's twenty-six session *Bible Timeline* series
for many years. As we went through this excellent program,
I could see that my parishioners were largely focused on the
intellectual and reading comprehension questions and not the
life application questions. I created an additional session at the
end—a relaxed potluck—as an opportunity to dig into their
experience of applying Scripture. During this time of fellowship, I asked the participants a simple question: how has going
through this Bible study impacted your relationship with Jesus
Christ? After a few moments of stunned silence, people began
to open up and share. Eventually this additional opportunity

became standard practice at our parish for any program, course, or speaking event.

If we want to shift the cultures in our parishes and dioceses, we'll have to move away from a mass-market approach to ministry and parish life, learn to accompany individuals on their spiritual journey toward God, and create structures at the parish and diocesan levels that allow for customized accompaniment of our people. That's a tall order, but Jesus has provided a model for how we might go about this.

Power to the People

The Gospels reveal that Jesus spent much of his time teaching, preaching, and healing the crowds of people who followed him. He did not, however, invest his life in the crowds to the same degree that he did with his twelve apostles. Even within that band of disciples, Scripture demonstrates, Jesus spent the greatest amount of time with Peter, James, and John.

This is a model for spiritual multiplication: Jesus invested himself particularly in twelve men, producing divine fruit within them. These men, in turn, spent their lives being Jesus for others, investing themselves and producing divine fruit through the power of the Holy Spirit. If we want to experience the release of fruitfulness and renewal within our parishes and dioceses, we will have to return to this model.

Sherry Weddell calls the Church to this exact value in *Fruitful Discipleship*: "At this moment in our history, we need to build a parish-literate missionary band of evangelizers whose primary work is to help individuals and families become mature disciples and fruit-bearing apostles."[26] We must move beyond our reliance on programs, tools, and resources and return to the art of personal discipling.

Parishes and dioceses invested in a paradigm of people recognize that authentic transformation and a life of discipleship emerge when we accompany people on their journey to Jesus. These parishes spend time, energy, and resources on raising up a generation of men and women who know how to walk with others into relationship with Christ. These missionary leaders understand their own identity in Christ as sons and daughters of God. They are equipped to share Jesus with others, and they possess a great desire to "sow into" the lives of others so that these others, in turn, can encounter the Lord Jesus and surrender their hearts to him.

This is precisely the work that my apostolate, M3 Ministries, does with parishes and dioceses. In the course of the last several years, we have seen firsthand how the presence of these missionary bands of evangelizers challenge the parish culture and bring a missionary perspective—not only into their worship of God and their daily lives but also into the meetings and plans of the parish community.

As we work alongside pastors, staff, pastoral leaders, and key volunteers, we equip men and women who

- possess a deep understanding of the Great Story of Salvation (the kerygma)—including how the gospel message applies to them and how their story and the Great Story intersect;
- demonstrate a desire to share the kerygma (the core gospel message) with others and walk alongside them into relationship with Christ;

- understand the spiritual journey toward discipleship and have experience listening to others to determine at what stage of discipleship or pre-discipleship a person might be;
- possess integrated knowledge of the evangelization process and can think about parish life through the lens of that process;
- can concretely invite someone to surrender their lives to Jesus; and
- demonstrate comfort with the power, presence, and person of the Holy Spirit and can partner with the Spirit to release the power of the kingdom of God in both natural and supernatural ways.

Of course, parishioners don't need to be formed in all these areas to be effective witnesses to Jesus. New disciples—and long-term followers of Christ whose lives have been reenergized by the Lord—can profoundly touch the lives of others in Jesus' name without the benefit of such a missionary formation. However, a parish or diocese that is rooted within a paradigm of people consciously chooses to raise up these kinds of missionary leaders, so that the missionary activity of the whole parish will bear greater fruit. In other words, leaders in a people-focused paradigm don't hold their people back from missionary activity until they complete all of the "necessary" formation; rather they seek to build up the missionary skills and identity of every parishioner, so that everyone can become more effective and fruitful in sharing Jesus with others.

In addition, leaders in a people-focused paradigm understand the value of linking programs, processes, and events along discipleship pathways. These communities ask themselves:

- What opportunities do we offer the unchurched to encounter the love of the Father in Jesus Christ?
- What ways do we have for someone to hear the gospel message and be accompanied into relationship with Christ?
- What ways do we have for people to grow into maturity as disciples of Jesus?
- In what ways do we equip our disciples to share Jesus with others and transform the world?
- And finally, do all of these things come together in a clear path, so that we can nurture, support, evaluate, and get better at the ways we walk with someone from being unchurched all the way through to missionary discipleship?

In my capacity as executive director of M3 Ministries, I've worked with the leaders of St. Francis de Sales Parish in Lake Zurich, Illinois, as they made this transition into a people-focused paradigm. When they initially brought me on, I spent time developing their leadership team, helping them create and embrace a vision, and raising up a first generation of missionary leaders in a formation process they called Equip. As their grasp of the vision spread and deepened, and the first generation of missionary leaders started to emerge, the leaders recognized that, if they wanted this focus on missionary leaders to be sustainable,

Elements of Living in a Paradigm of Programs

- Parish sees the "right" program as the primary solution to problems or the primary driver of engagement.
- Parish functions under the belief that good programs will make disciples.
- Parish tends to hire in favor of administrative and operational strengths and gifts, often valuing programmatic execution over spiritual fruitfulness.
- Parish doesn't link programs along a clear pathway of discipleship or mission.
- Programs are executed with little personal follow-up or recognition of the importance of the individual spiritual journey and response to grace.

Elements of Living in a Paradigm of People

- Parish understands that discipleship emerges out of a sustained experience of accompaniment (that is, people make disciples).
- Parish raises up parishioners who are equipped and desire to accompany others.
- Parish links programs, events, and processes strategically, to create clear pathways to discipleship.
- Parish combines the right programs with the right people, so that this accompaniment bears the greatest fruits.

they needed to help them grow in even deeper maturity as disciples. During the second year, we began a formation process geared toward maturing disciples, which the folks at St. Francis de Sales named Build.

Now that we are three years into this journey, the parish is about to realize its long-term goal of launching the Alpha Course. Alpha is a multi-week series of gatherings designed for the unchurched and those interested in exploring questions of faith. Alpha allows them to wrestle with the deep questions of life and hear the kerygma proclaimed in a safe, nonthreatening environment.

With the advent of the Alpha Course, this parish now has the major building blocks of its discipleship pathways fleshed out: Alpha, for the unchurched and those not yet in a relationship with Jesus; Build, geared toward those who are enquiring or who have made a decision to follow Jesus but are not yet rooted in the various disciplines of discipleship; and Equip, a comprehensive process for preparing disciples to become missionary leaders established in the art of accompaniment. The leadership of the parish is also in the process of creating small and mid–sized groups that will help nurture individuals who are not quite ready to move into Build or Equip.

Although St. Francis de Sales Parish is still in the early days of this transition, the presence of passionate disciples and missionary leaders with a clear vision is already having an effect. This parish and others like it demonstrate that if parishes and dioceses can release their death grip on programmatic responses to the crises we currently face and embrace a people-focused paradigm, we will see more and more renewal in our communities.

8

From Avoidance to Accountability

Although holiness is one of the four marks of the Church, the Church is made up of fallible, broken human beings. Because we are all less than holy, our interactions are colored by our brokenness. As we have discussed, human organizations are a lot like living organisms. Just as pathogens can cause serious illness within living organisms, dysfunctions, personality issues, broken relationships, and a host of other interpersonal issues can cause sickness within organizations, including the Church.

In the natural world, health is essentially linked to growth. Fr. James Mallon underscored this point in a video interview with Peter Herbeck, director of missions for Renewal Ministries. "You're a father," Fr. James said to Peter. "Did you ever sit your children down and solemnly lecture them to grow? No. You kept them healthy, and you fed them, and they grew all by themselves."[27]

In other words, healthy things grow.

This is true in the world of business too. Patrick Lencioni, one of the most sought-after organizational consultants in the United States, contends that "the health of an organization provides the context for strategy, finance, marketing, technology, and everything that happens within it, which is why it is the single greatest factor determining an organization's success."[28]

The Church isn't simply a human organization, of course, and God has equipped us and given us his grace as a Church to be fruitful. If we cooperate with that grace individually and as a people, our organizational health will move us toward a positive disposition by which we can receive and share the supernatural life of God. Organizational health, therefore, affects every area of parish life, both administrative and ministerial. A healthy parish will bear fruit; an unhealthy parish will find its fruit-bearing blocked and blunted.

Unfortunately, in my years of ministry, I have seen that dysfunction within parish and diocesan organizations tends be the norm. Leadership breakdowns and organizational issues have caused real human trauma in the life of our Church. At its most extreme, this dysfunction leads not only to sexual abuse but also to the institutional cover-up of such abuse.

All human organizations possess some level of dysfunction, of course, but certain principles and cultural values perpetuate dysfunction. One of the key culprits in reinforcing this dysfunction is the paradigm of avoidance.

Playing the Avoidance Game

In a paradigm of avoidance, leaders dodge difficult, forthright conversations about such things as performance or whether a ministry is bearing fruit. They do this because they want to be nice and don't want to hurt anyone's feelings. This is a natural human trait: most of us want to be liked; we don't want to be a source of pain for others. Further, many of us in leadership positions in the Church have been trained to bring healing to others and to nurture them. But when we combine the desire to be nice with the instinct to heal and nurture, we have a recipe for avoidance.

Let's face it, most pastors didn't answer the call to priesthood because they wanted to handle interpersonal conflict or navigate organizational challenges—and we probably didn't sign up for that stuff either when we jumped in to volunteer or work at our parish. One pastor confided that he felt the seminary formed him primarily to be a chaplain, to care for the spiritual needs of his community. "But," he said, referring to a group of motivated parishioners who wanted to see the parish renewed, "they are trying to make me into a *leader*."

This tendency to avoid conflict, though natural, is unhealthy, especially if taken to extremes. One parish staff member I know reported that her pastor would simply not come into the office if there was a situation that involved interpersonal conflict. "One time," she said, "my pastor needed to have a difficult conversation with me. I'm a pretty intuitive person, and I sensed that he was upset, but he spent two weeks finding excuses to be away from the office, both during the days and in the evenings! Finally I couldn't take it anymore. I called him up and said, 'Obviously, Father, you have something that you need to talk with me about, but you just don't want to. The only thing is, if I don't know what I'm doing wrong, I can't fix it. Can we meet for lunch tomorrow and talk about this?'"

Avoidance can manifest itself at staff, pastoral council, or finance council meetings. Perhaps the pastor or another leader puts forth an idea or suggests a particular policy decision. In an avoidance-focused paradigm, those who have problems with the proposal rarely make their objections known. Rather they just nod their heads and return to their office after the meeting determined to resist whatever strategic direction was put forth. Or they gather with like-minded individuals and quietly complain. I sometimes think we have raised passive-aggressive behavior to an art form in the Church.

I've also been in meetings where there is an eight-hundred-pound gorilla in the room—an incident from the past, for example—that needs to be addressed, but the meeting concludes without anyone mentioning it. I've seen pastors blow up at a staff member or a volunteer during meetings; I've watched two people get into a verbal fight. And in every case, no one in the meeting dealt with it; they just swept it under the rug.

On the surface, the paradigm of avoidance keeps the peace; but in reality, it leads to a lack of accountability and to sustained dysfunction, bitterness, woundedness, and poor morale. Organizational speaker Peter Bromberg puts it this way: "When we avoid difficult conversations, we trade short-term discomfort for long-term dysfunction."[29] Your best and most committed performers will soon understand that their hard work doesn't matter. They'll become frustrated as they see that no one deals with people who slack off in their jobs, and no one addresses challenging issues.

Refusing to have difficult conversations also sends the signal that you don't care about people. Think of the situation of a staff member or key volunteer who has been in a particular area of ministry for decades but hasn't been bearing fruit. (I often see this.) In a paradigm of avoidance, it's likely that no one has ever addressed those issues with that volunteer and therefore never given that person a chance to grow and improve. Now, what happens when a new pastor comes in and simply fires that individual? For twenty years that person has been serving in ministry, no one has said anything to indicate there might be a problem with their service—and suddenly they're asked to leave. It's not only unfortunate; it's also unjust.

Living in a paradigm of avoidance can also negatively impact the growth and renewal of your parish. Leaders with an avoidance mindset often won't press forward on a strategic direction or execute a solid vision, because it might mean having difficult conversations with unpleasant consequences for particular people.

For example, I once worked with a pastor on the East Coast who acknowledged that he didn't have the right employees in the right positions in his parish. After spending time with his staff and observing the parish, I created five different organizational charts. One chart represented how the parish was currently organized. Another detailed what the organizational structure of the parish should actually be in a perfect world. The remaining three charts contained organizational structures that were somewhere between the current structure and the perfect one.

The pastor thanked me and acknowledged that he needed to make changes. I checked back with him and was stunned to discover, nearly eighteen months later, that he had yet to make a single change to his parish structure. The reason? He didn't want to deal with the parish secretary, who would most likely explode with anger over the proposed changes—*even though he recognized that the parish secretary represented the single biggest obstacle to the cultural change he was trying to bring about at the parish.*

Thriving in Accountability

In contrast to those in the paradigm of avoidance, leaders working out of a paradigm of accountability see that it is the role of leadership to be concerned at every level with both the pastoral care of individuals and fruitful effectiveness. As a result, these leaders embrace difficult conversations; they confront reality, seeing this as an act of charity and service to the whole community. They build habits of what business leader and consultant Kim Scott calls "radical candor," an approach to communication that combines the two dimensions of caring personally for others and of demonstrating that through a willingness to challenge directly.[30] This approach to radical candor is an embodiment of Paul's exhortation to live (and speak) "the truth in love" (Ephesians 4:15).

In order to really embrace radical candor, leaders must learn how to embrace conflict. We aren't talking about power struggles and the playing out of our own brokenness within relationships. Pat Lencioni describes it this way:

> [T]he conflict I am referring to here is not the nasty kind that centers around people or personalities. Rather, it is what I call productive ideological conflict, the willingness to disagree, even passionately when necessary, around important issues and decisions that must be made.[31]

Reaching that kind of productive ideological conflict requires that leadership teams and functioning groups move to a place of trust. If there are personality conflicts within the team or group, members must address these lovingly. By dealing with these forthrightly and practicing the principles of radical candor as they grow in trust with each other, these groups build the essential habits of communication that are the building blocks of a paradigm of accountability. Kim Scott describes what can happen when organizations embrace such a candid approach to communication:

Radical candor builds trust and opens the door for the kind of communication that helps you achieve the results you're aiming for. . . . It turns out that when people trust you and believe that you care about them, they are much more likely to 1) accept and act on your praise and criticism; 2) tell you what they really think about what *you* are doing well and, more importantly, not doing well; 3) engage in this same behavior with one another . . . ; 4) embrace their role on the team; and 5) focus on *getting results.*[32]

Radical candor is infectious: it spreads throughout an organization like a good virus, bringing change and helping the transition into a paradigm of accountability. It builds up trust between people. Leaders who embrace radical candor and thus are rooted in an accountability-focused paradigm willingly hold themselves and each other to agreed-upon standards of performance and common values. In an accountable organization, leaders will call each other out when necessary, and though the experience may not be pleasant for the one who needs a wake-up call, everyone understands that this is done out of love and respect.

I experienced what life in a paradigm of accountability might be like several years ago when I led a parish mission for a community in Canada. The pastor of that parish asked the director of communications—I'll call her Mary—to bring me to the church about a half hour before my mission talk was scheduled. One thing led to another, and Mary delivered me to the parish at 6:50 and not 6:30, a full twenty minutes late!

Now, the pastor of that parish was a wonderful man and an amazing priest—but he had no poker face whatsoever. By the time he and I were able to talk—shortly before my presentation—I could see that he was upset. His intention in pulling me aside was simply to encourage me. What he said were things like "We love you" and "We want you to just be yourself." Because of my own family background, however, I am acutely aware of the emotional state of other people, and so I interpreted his words through the lens of his anger. What he said was "We want you to just be yourself," but what I heard was "I don't think you are being authentic"— ten minutes before I was supposed to speak to a full house and lead them in prayer!

Needless to say, I freaked out and went to Mary to tell her what happened. I should have realized I was in a different kind of parish when she put her hand on my shoulder, looked me straight in the eye, and said, "Well, you and the pastor are both grown men, so how about you talk to him directly about what you experienced rather than coming to me?" That shocked me enough to snap me out of my funk and allow me to proceed confidently with my mission talk.

After the evening wrapped up, a number of people were still hanging around in the church. I was surprised when Mary walked up to the pastor and, in front of me and a few leaders who were gathered together, spoke to him. She apologized for not getting me to the church at the agreed-upon time. She not only took complete responsibility for her mistake but also told her pastor the concrete things she was going to do to make sure nothing like that happened again.

But Mary wasn't finished.

My mouth nearly fell open as she continued talking: "And, Father, I need you to understand that you can't talk to a speaker

Elements of Living in a Paradigm of Avoidance

- Difficult conversations—about fruit, performance, or behavior—are avoided because "we don't want to hurt other people's feelings."
- Disagreements are buried or misaligned with strategic direction or proposals during meetings, in order to keep the peace.
- Eight-hundred-pound gorillas lurk over conversations and decisions.
- Parishioners, leaders, and staff experience frustration, poor morale, and dysfunction because issues are not addressed.
- There is no forward movement on a strategic direction or execution of a solid vision because of perceived difficulties of change or consequences for a person or group in the parish or diocese

Elements of Living in a Paradigm of Accountability

- Leaders at every level see their roles in both pastoral care of individuals and fruitful effectiveness of mission.
- Individuals embrace radical candor as a primary mode of communication.
- Conflict is understood as a catalyst for positive change, growth, and transformation.
- Passive aggressiveness, sacred cows, and resistance to direction are not tolerated.
- Leaders do not shy away from strategic decisions in fear that the decisions might upset others.

in an agitated state ten minutes before he's scheduled to speak and not expect it's going to affect him negatively, so I need you to not do that again!" Clearly, this was a different kind of parish, I thought, as I watched the pastor accept Mary's apology and accept her correction.

In a paradigm of accountability, priests and deacons are not excused from accountability and the expectation of positive behavior and performance. Parishes and dioceses that embrace accountability don't shy away from making hard decisions— even if these have major consequences for people, positions, and groups within the community. Joined together by a bond of respect and trust, leaders, staff, and key volunteers walk the road together. Conflict isn't the enemy in a paradigm of accountability but rather a catalyst for change. "Where there is trust," Patrick Lencioni writes, "conflict becomes nothing but the pursuit of truth, an attempt to find the best possible answer."[33]

This isn't a radical, revolutionary call for change in the Church's theology but rather a simple acknowledgment that we must approach leadership, administration, and governance in a different way. If we can release candor into our organizations, in the context of trust, we will receive the transformative grace of God that allows us to be channels of his love for our parishioners and, most important, for the civic community around us.

PART THREE

MOVING
FORWARD

9

Wrapping Our Arms around Change

Cultural change is hard.

Setting the stage for the renewal of a parish or diocese, helping Catholics envision and embrace new ways of "being" Catholic, and creating structures and processes that support a new culture—all of it is hard. When the smoke clears from the latest conference and the excitement of new ideas crashes into the ongoing treadmill of emails, meetings, scheduling, and other hallmarks of maintenance—that's when the tsunami of feeling overwhelmed falls upon pastors, staff, councils, and key volunteers.

How will we ever do this? Where do we even start? I'm not cut out for this! What if people leave? How will we afford this? How will the bishop react?

These are concerns that run through the minds of many parish leaders when they start to contemplate parish renewal. These questions and worries, left unchecked, can lead to a kind of organizational paralysis, whether through indecision or a Tower-of-Babel-like influx of voices and opinions.

It's kind of like living with an eight-year-old. Let me explain.

My daughter, Siena, is eight, and living with an eight-year-old child is a lot like living with a tornado. No sooner have we corralled her to clean up her room, gather up her dolls from around the house, and organize her closet than another outbreak of tornadic winds assaults our domicile. We turn around and Siena's room is somehow even messier than before, and her dolls have once again made what seems like a frenetic pilgrimage to the various corners of our living space. There are days when we stare at the array of toys, collectibles, clothes, crayons, and crafts that lie strewn about the house—and we feel paralyzed. When it comes to the cleanup, we don't know where to start! It isn't until we wrap our arms around the problem, breaking it down into its component parts, that we can formulate a response.

The same is true of parish transformation and cultural renewal. Often, the sheer amount of work that needs to be done can overcome our excitement and passion, shutting down our ability to move forward. However, if we can wrap our arms around the need for change, elevating our vision so that we can view the need from a vantage point above the surrounding confusion, we will discover the steps that we should take. It reminds me of the adage "How do you eat an elephant? One bite at a time!"

In her book *Move*, business leader and consultant Patty Azzarello reveals an effective formula for change that has helped businesses and organizations experience renewal and cultural transformation. This "change formula," created by David Gleicher in 1969, highlights the components necessary for lasting transformation. The Gleicher Formula, as it is sometimes called, is expressed mathematically:

$$D \times V \times F > R$$

Spelled out, the factors are

D = Dissatisfaction with Current State

V = Vision of the Future

F = First Concrete Steps to Get There

R = Resistance to Change (what I have defined previously as cultural inertia)

Azzarello explains that "this equation says that if any one of the things on the left [D, V, or F] is zero, the resistance, no matter how small, will not be overcome, and the change will not happen."[34]

In other words, change will happen when dissatisfaction, a vision for the future, and a plan for initial steps to get to the future are strong enough to overcome the resistance to change. In short, organizational change requires a combination of dissatisfaction with the current reality, a clear vision of what could or should be, and a plan to get there. The more real and practical those are, the greater the chance that the organization will break through cultural inertia and resistance and go on to experience real and lasting transformation. On the other hand, the more vague, diffuse, and unclear any of those things are, the greater the chance for failure.

I Can't Get No Satisfaction!

The first component of the Gleicher Equation is dissatisfaction with the current state. Although parishes and dioceses are becoming increasingly aware of the critical problems we face because of a lack of discipleship, not every pastor, leader, or key volunteer wants to go through an intense process of reevaluation, reflection, and planned change. A popular saying, currently attributed to Tony Robbins, a motivational speaker and self-help expert, sheds some light on this reality. It goes something like this: "Change happens when the pain of staying the same is greater than the pain of change."

ABLAZE

In some places, the pain of staying the same is not yet greater than the perceived pain of change. This is especially true in places where there is growth through immigration, such as in a growing metropolitan area like Houston; an acceptable level of resources, as in a wealthy parish; or the presence of a Catholic cultural stronghold, as in certain parts of the eastern United States. These factors can mask the very real issues that we face. In addition, our current crisis of declining membership in North America and Europe obscures the reality that many of our people do not understand that there is much more to parish life and being Catholic than simply attending Mass on Sunday.

As pastoral leaders and engaged volunteers, we need to help many of our brothers and sisters begin to see the depths of our faith, those things that they are not currently equipped to see because of their Catholic cultural lens. This is why it is so critical for leaders to make the five essential paradigm shifts named in this book. We need a generation of Catholics who can break open these paradigm shifts for others, align parish and diocesan life with the new paradigms, and accompany our people as they make these shifts themselves.

I'm taking it for granted that, because you are reading this book, you are dissatisfied with the way your current parish is living out its missionary mandate and you want to be part of that generation for others. In order to help you wrap your arms around the task before you, the rest of this book will provide a basic, easy-to-understand approach to parish renewal. That approach looks something like this:

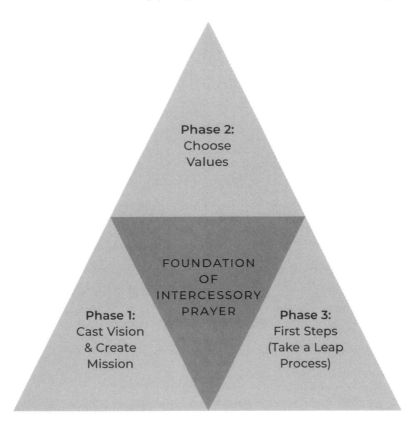

Phase 2:
Choose
Values

FOUNDATION
OF
INTERCESSORY
PRAYER

Phase 1:
Cast Vision
& Create
Mission

Phase 3:
First Steps
(Take a Leap
Process)

Laying a Foundation of Prayer

Before we spend time looking at the three components of cultural change, it is critical that we talk about the most important aspect of parish transformation: prayer. If you belong to a parish whose leaders want to begin this transformation process—especially if they've been spinning their wheels for a while—or if you are the lone voice in the wilderness crying out for change, the most effective way to ensure that transformation occurs is to lay a solid foundation of prayer.

Leaders should create opportunities for leadership teams, volunteers, and parishioners to pray together for the renewal of the parish. As I wrote in a chapter I contributed to in *Becoming a Parish of Intentional Disciples*:

> I often describe intercessory prayer as God's "Shock and Awe Campaign," because the fruit of individual and corporate intercession is often an overwhelming display of God's mercy, providence, and deliverance that changes the spiritual climate around a person or a place and transforms situations. Intercessory prayer disrupts the "infrastructure" of the Enemy, by which I mean it weakens and destroys the network of lies, fear, intimidation, and confusion—the tools and strategies used by Satan to keep persons and situations away from God's peace, clarity, and redeeming love. In changing the spiritual climate around a person or community, this kind of prayer helps till the soil of the heart and prepares it to receive the seed of the Gospel.[35]

In addition to engaging the whole parish to pray for renewal, leaders should identify their key intercessors, those men and women who not only have a passion to pray for others but also possess a charism for intercessory prayer. Ask these intercessors to pray that the dissatisfaction parishioners have with the current state of parish life would increase (this is a holy dissatisfaction if oriented toward the renewal of our baptismal mission). They should also pray that hearts become open to renewal and that parishioners embrace new approaches to parish life.

Continue this prayer throughout the renewal process. Your intercessors should bring specific needs before the Lord, but they should also ask the Father to reveal those things for which he wants them to pray. Meet regularly with this team of intercessors, and listen to their feedback. In this way, your community will be calling on the power of God to facilitate your parish renewal. This must be the foundation of your efforts!

In the next chapter, we'll explore the next component of the change equation—visioning.

10

Aligning with Vision and Values

I have a terrible sense of direction.

My mom said that when I was growing up, I was the only person she knew who could get lost just riding his bike around the block. To this day, I am deeply grateful for the inventors of the GPS, and I thank God for its presence on my phone. If I know my destination, I can plug that into my phone and receive detailed instructions on how to get there.

A similar thing is true when it comes to parish renewal. Leadership teams that invest time and energy in building a clear sense of mission and vision have a greater chance of achieving it.

Yogi Berra got it right in this regard. Yogi was an all-star major-league baseball player, as well as a manager for the New York Yankees and New York Mets. Yogi was famous for his unintentional witticisms, which some people call "Yogi-isms." One such Yogi-ism revolves around the necessity for vision. "If you don't know where you're going," Yogi used to say, "you'll end up someplace else."[36] In other words, it's hard to get somewhere if you don't know where you want to go.

One of the most powerful cures for leadership paralysis in the face of an overwhelming task such as parish renewal is a clear understanding of the purpose of an organization—why do we exist?—and its destination: where are we headed? Trying to renew the parish out of a sense of desperation or in an effort to keep the doors open is not a sufficient vision. The survival instinct is useful for kicking off frenetic activity. It does little, however, to foster a disciplined approach to reorganizing parish life in order to yield more fruit. As Patrick Lencioni has said: "Employees in every organization, and at every level, need to know that at the heart of what they do lies something grand and aspirational."[37] That knowledge inspires and energizes members of the organization, and it also acts as a North Star guiding all strategic decisions. Ultimately a solid vision yields operational impact.

Returning to the Gleicher Formula ($D \times V \times F > R$), where D = dissatisfaction with current state, V = vision of the future, F = first concrete steps to get there, and R = resistance to change, parish leaders who want to see parish renewal must create clear vision and mission statements in order to invest the variable V (vision of the future) with the greatest value possible. This is why we discussed such statements at length in chapter 3.

Although it is always good to begin with the end in mind, in my experience working with parishes, I have found that it is sometimes easier to walk people through a process of visioning and missioning by exploring the mission first—why do we exist?—and then moving on to vision. The reason: many Catholics do not understand the overall purpose of the Church, and therefore they cannot create a vision—or cast a vision, as we sometimes say—that expresses the fullness of the Church's identity. Getting to the root of the Church's mission creates clarity for parishes and dioceses around their own mission. That clarity, in turn, helps them create a sufficiently broad and deep vision for their community.

Mission and Vision Statements Pro Tip

In the creation of your parish or diocesan mission statement, you don't need to start from scratch. Jesus Christ has already commissioned the Church, as we see in the Gospel of Matthew: "Go . . . and make disciples of all nations" (Matthew 28:19). *As you gather your leaders to explore what your community's mission should be, this Great Commission is a place to start. It is also a great jumping-off point for creating a vision.*

What might it look like if your parish or diocese began to bear fruit living out the Great Commission? When I accompany communities, I generally ask their leaders to imagine that they have been fulfilling the Great Commission for ten years and to list the details for what that might look like. From there I work with them on distilling that future snapshot into a succinct vision. (You can check back to chapter 3 for specific examples of vision statements.)

Oh, Behave!

The next phase in this basic approach to parish renewal is to identify key values. Remember that values are the building blocks of culture. According to Pat Lencioni:

> The answer to the question, *How do we behave?* is embodied in an organization's core values, which should provide the ultimate guide for employee behavior at all levels. This . . . is an area that Collins and Porras addressed in *Built to Last*. In their research, they found that enduring, successful companies adhered strictly

to a fundamental set of principles that guided their behaviors and decisions over time, preserving the essence of the organization.[38]

Your leadership group should create a set of values that harmonize with your vision and mission statements. If they do that well, these values will guide them as they execute variable F in the Gleicher Formula. This will give your community another lens through which to evaluate actions and activities throughout this process.

Choosing Values Pro Tip

Again, you do not have to start from scratch in the process of identifying and choosing values. The five paradigm shifts covered in this book represent a broad-based (or macro) value. You could decide to simply adopt them and move forward from there. Or your leadership group could drill down on each of the five paradigms and produce one or two more specific values that they want to embrace. Whether you work out a set of values from scratch, drill down to produce some from the five paradigms, or just adopt the five paradigms whole cloth, the most important thing is that your leaders, staff, and key volunteers understand what these values mean and fully commit to them!

Alignment: It's Not Just for Tires

As you journey through this process of renewal, your leaders must be in alignment—with your vision, mission, values, pastoral strategy, and each other. Alignment is more than agreement; it is an expression of organizational and personal integrity. At its best, "alignment is common beliefs and concerted action in collective pursuit of a clear result."[39] In an aligned parish, the vision, mission, values, structures, processes, strategy, and execution connect to each other and are consistent with each other.

We see this expressed in a Latin maxim often used to describe the life and activity of the Church: *Lex orandi, lex credendi, lex vivendi.* Roughly translated, it means, "The law of prayer is the law of belief, which is the law of life." In other words, there is an integrity between how the Church worships, what she believes, and how she tries to live. That same principle must be lived out organizationally by your leaders at every level of the parish or diocese and in every phase of the renewal process.

For example, when choosing values, every leader in your leadership group must be willing to live out those values and commit to them. One sign that an organization has successfully achieved alignment around their values is

> when it will allow itself to be punished for living those values and when it accepts the fact that employees will sometimes take those values too far.[40]

Let's say that your parish leadership agrees to embrace the paradigm of encounter as a key value. The director of religious education, therefore, looks for ways to foster an encounter with Jesus for families in the parish religious education program. In addition to the regular array of religious education activities, she might require parents and children in the First Communion program to attend a retreat focused on the basic gospel proclamation. Families operating out of current paradigms may resist such an "imposition" and choose to send their children to a neighboring parish's program. Would your pastor and the leadership of the parish be willing to see fewer children in the religious education program and therefore less revenue in the budget because the DRE chose to live out that value? In aligned parishes, the answer would be yes.

Without this alignment of values, the scope and speed of renewal in your community will be dramatically slowed and, if this misalignment is acute enough, possibly stopped. If your leaders are not aligned with your values, the very best you will get is "compliance, but not commitment; involvement, but not investment; and progress, but not lasting performance."[41] Chances are, you'll end up with a lot worse.

Again, this alignment must extend not only to values but throughout the whole linked chain of the renewal process in order to have operational influence. As Larry Bossidy and Ram Charan explain in their book *Confronting Reality*:

> Real results do not come from making bold announcements about how the organization will change. They come from thoughtful, committed leaders who understand the details of an initiative, anticipate its consequences for the organization, make sure their people can achieve it, put their personal weight behind it, and communicate its urgency to everyone.[42]

Such commitment and proactive execution only come from leaders who are fully aligned and are willing to follow through on a strategic plan that flows from vision, mission, and values. They do so even if it means that their personal influence, area of responsibility, or ministry might be reduced in importance or shifted to a new focus.

This happened to me. I was the head of marketing and sales for a startup company when a much larger company bought it. The new parent company had a long history of direct sales that differed from my startup's approach and that had shaped the overall culture of the new company. It made sense to align with their core values. I have many competencies as a business executive, but direct sales is not one of them. I was passionate about the company I worked for, however, and I wanted it to succeed in its mission. Therefore I set about redeveloping our sales and marketing teams into direct sales teams, working with our parent company to find the right people to lead those teams in the future.

Basically I was working myself out of a job. I could have stalled, fought the tide of change, even sabotaged the parent company's efforts in an attempt to milk my paycheck as long as possible, until I either defeated the initiative or landed my next gig. However, I was so aligned with the vision, mission, and strategy of our growing startup that it never even occurred to me to do so.

Key Indicators of Misalignment

Misalignment breeds dysfunction, creates operational inefficiencies, blunts effectiveness, damages fruit, and hurts people. It has real consequences for real individuals. In *Change the Culture, Change the Game*, Connors and Smith detail several signs of misalignment. These include

- People remain silent and don't voice their opinion when you call for a decision.

- You keep being surprised by the actions people take because they are inconsistent with the agreed-upon direction.
- You don't see tangible progress on an issue when by all rights you should be moving forward throughout the organization.
- In meetings, people keep bringing up issues that you thought were resolved.
- People complain, make excuses, and blame others for lack of progress.
- You observe a lack of ownership and enthusiasm for implementing an established course of action.
- People voice disagreement with a decision or a direction that has already been taken.[43]

Although these signs are written from the perspective of someone who is a manager or key leader, you don't have to be one to recognize misalignment. If you are not in a direct position of authority or influence to deal with signs that you see in your parish, you can still contribute to changing the culture and fostering alignment by taking the time to understand the vision, mission, values, and strategy of your church community. Then make a deliberate decision to bring yourself into alignment and to live those values out in your pocket of community life—no matter how limited or minor that might seem to you.

Dealing with a Misaligned Leader

One of the key questions that people ask when I work with parishes or dioceses is "What do we do with a misaligned leader?" It is a difficult question with an even more difficult answer: *You absolutely must replace a leader who either can't or won't align themselves with the vision, mission, values, and strategy of a parish or diocese—regardless of the inconvenience, cost, or negative effect that might stem from that leader's departure.*

The challenge here is that misaligned leaders rarely announce themselves publicly. They often hide their resistance. They will use whatever influence, authority, and resources they have to undermine initiatives, rally an underground resistance, and cast doubt on other leaders. They might see themselves as acting on behalf of the community, but regardless of their intentions, a misaligned leader will present an obstacle to parish renewal.

In order to deal with a misaligned leader and bring them out into the open, a leader with sufficient authority or standing should engage that person in a conversation marked by radical candor. This leader should ask questions that get to the heart of what is going on: "It seems you're not excited about some of the values we agreed on in that meeting; would that be a fair understanding of your perspective?" "We've all been working toward reshaping our ministries according to the mission and values we adopted as a parish, but there doesn't seem to be much movement in your area. What are the issues that you are facing, and how can I help?"

Once it is clear that a leader is misaligned, it is essential that you give them opportunities to bring themselves into alignment. Whoever has responsibility for that misaligned leader must help them create clear objectives that will signal alignment and then hold them accountable to agree to and complete those objectives within a certain time frame.

For example, let's say that you're the adult faith formation director at your parish, and you have been given responsibility for the bereavement ministry, which is led by a volunteer. As a way of living out your parish's commitment to the paradigm of intentional faith, you've asked all your teams to begin each meeting with fifteen minutes of prayer and reflection on the upcoming week's Sunday Gospel. You've worked with all of your ministry leaders to form them in how to lead these reflections, but two months have gone by and you've heard that the bereavement team hasn't started doing them. Word has also come back to you that the head of the bereavement team has said that they don't have time to do all that "prayer stuff" because the team is too busy.

After you have had direct conversations with the bereavement team leader and confirmed that he is misaligned, it's time to be pretty specific. The best thing to do is to reiterate the importance of the fifteen-minute prayer time, make it clear that it will start by a certain date, and then offer that person any assistance they need to make it happen. If after the agreed-upon time it still hasn't happened, you should have another conversation and see if the source of the delay is still misalignment or something else. If it does turn out to be misalignment, you should begin the process of finding another bereavement team leader.

I can already hear the objections: "What if I'm in a small parish, and I can't find anyone else?" "What if he has led that ministry since the time of Methuselah?" "I can't take those actions, as it would most likely hurt him and make our relationship awkward."

All of those objections might be true—and it still doesn't change the reality that this leader must be replaced. If your goal is parish renewal and cultural change, there are no other options. Cultural inertia is simply too strong a force. Not replacing misaligned leaders is like trying to race a car with your foot on the brake: you won't go very fast, and you'll burn a lot of rubber along the way.

In fact, dealing forthrightly with a misaligned leader is a profound act of charity. As the new culture you want to see starts forming around you, misaligned leaders will become even more frustrated and unhappy. That can spill into their personal lives and their relationship with God. Helping misaligned leaders disengage from a job or area of parish life that does not fulfill them and that actually causes them pain and frustration demonstrates real care and concern for them as persons. This is even more so if we can do this with compassion and help them find an opportunity somewhere that might be a better fit for them. In addition, replacing misaligned leaders is also an act of charity for the entire community, who will experience greater fruitfulness when the number of aligned leaders and key volunteers increases.

The effect of alignment on a community is significant. Once you have this alignment around vision, mission, and values, you can move to phase three of this simple renewal process: taking the first steps. To help you move forward, the next chapter details a specific six-step process to help you take a leap into cultural change.

11

Taking the First Steps
(Pastoral Planning)

I am a huge *Star Wars* fan. (Don't worry, I also love *Star Trek*.) I have loved *Star Wars* ever since my cousin Doug took me to see *Episode IV: A New Hope* back in 1977. At one point in that movie, the main character, Luke Skywalker, starts his training in the ways of the Force, guided by the Jedi master Ben "Obi Wan" Kenobi. Obi Wan blindfolds Luke and has him try to block laser blasts from a remote drone. Predictably, the clueless young apprentice gets hit many times, until Obi-Wan instructs him on how to use the Force. After some trial and error, Luke manages to block several shots from the drone. Excitedly, Luke tells his new master that he could almost see the drone with the power of the Force. Obi-Wan, obviously delighted in his apprentice, responds, "That's good. You've taken your first step into a larger world."

As we head into phase three of our simple roadmap for transformation—take the first steps—we are indeed stepping into the larger world of real cultural change and parish renewal. Here we move from articulating a vision and mission, and we enter into action. Like Luke Skywalker, we will make some missteps, and we'll receive bumps and bruises along the way. Because of this, our journey of renewal can seem overwhelming and even frightening. But it is also filled with great wonders and joy as we begin to discover possibilities and experience realities that go beyond anything we imagined.

God's dream for our parishes and dioceses, his desire for fruit, and his plans are greater than anything we could come up with on our own. When we start to surrender our own hopes and dreams for our communities and begin to align with his, amazing things happen.

But it's risky.

Acknowledging our dissatisfaction and creating solid vision and mission statements is one thing. Building pastoral plans that incarnate those statements and using them to make decisions that directly affect the life of flesh-and-blood communities—that's something entirely different. This goes beyond talk and becomes doing. This is where the sandals meet the road.

The presence of a strategic plan in any organization implies a particular focus of resources—time, money, and attention. The same is true of strategic pastoral plans. Currently many of our parishes and dioceses function like boutique communities, with an array of ministries, events, and services based on the interests and needs of members. Someone wants to start a particular ministry, and if there is any interest at all from other parishioners, and if they can find a staff to champion the idea, lo and behold, that ministry springs into being.

Communities guided by a strategic pastoral plan, however, use a different set of criteria to organize their life. A strategic pastoral plan declares what, when, and how the parish or diocese will invest its resources in order to best live out its mission and realize its vision.

An effective strategic pastoral plan also provides leadership with clear principles *to help them decide what to stop doing and what not to start doing—what opportunities to avoid.* The work of parish renewal isn't something that we can do in addition to all the other activities of our community. As I often say to the dioceses and parishes that I accompany, "You cannot change the culture of your community in the free time you have from living out your current culture."

In other words, parish renewal and cultural change are an intentional choice that shapes the life of your community, and they demand real focus. If you want to experience real renewal in your parish or diocese, you will need to let some areas of your community's life lie fallow, not pursuing them for several years at least. This will entail making difficult decisions about ending some events, traditions, ministries, and activities that are popular, long-standing, and doing good in your community. In the context of gardening, it's called weeding and pruning; both are designed to maximize the fruitfulness of the seeds that are taking root in the soil.

Of course, people are not weeds, and our communities aren't made up of plants. The harsh reality is, however, that if you want to embrace this path of renewal and start organizing parish life along the five paradigm shifts, you will end up hurting and angering some of your people—many of whom are wonderful, kind, trusting, generous folks, and all of whom are beloved children of God. *There is no avoiding this reality—and the desire to try to please and appease everyone can destroy a community's opportunity to experience renewal.*

This is, perhaps, the single biggest obstacle to a fruitful phase three. Pastors and pastoral leaders who see themselves primarily as chaplains, focused on the spiritual needs of their community members, will balk at this reality and resist making decisions that upset anyone. This, of course, creates, nurtures, and sustains a paradigm of avoidance. There will come a time in this phase of the journey, however, when pastoral leaders will have to make a choice between something that supports the old paradigms of the parish and something that supports the new paradigms out of which they want to live. It is always easier to choose the actions that favor the current culture, because these make the fewest waves.

On this journey of renewal, as we have seen, you will not be able to keep everybody. Though we do our best to walk with those who are confused, upset, and angry about the choices we are making, *some people either do not want to or cannot deal with the changes that renewal demands, and we must honor their freedom and let them go.* If we believe that God desires the transformation we are working toward and that it will bring about a greater experience of the love and mercy of God for the world, then we cannot allow this renewal to be held hostage by the resistance of others.

Remember, even Jesus couldn't keep all of his disciples. In chapter 6 of the Gospel of John, Jesus declares that his body is true food and his blood true drink. Scripture informs us that on hearing this, many of his followers left. Jesus didn't call after those who were abandoning him, offering to change his teaching or approach. Rather, he looked at the twelve disciples gathered around him and asked, "Do you also want to leave?" (John 6:67).

Pastoral leaders, staff, parish council members, and key volunteers who are not prepared to follow through on strategic plans will be unable to help foster renewal. But the good news is that a clear, well-defined, and simple strategic pastoral plan can make it easier for leaders at all levels to do so.

Creating the Plan

A strategic pastoral plan focuses the resources and attention of the community on actions, activities, and events that actually bear fruit in relation to the making, maturing, and missioning of disciples of Jesus. At their best, these plans create the foundation for what I and many of my colleagues call "discipleship pathways." These are a linked series of strategically chosen processes and activities designed to meet people where they are in the spiritual journey and lead them into missionary discipleship.

It reminds me of my days in the Boy Scouts of America.

I entered the Boy Scouts at age ten and spent eight years with that organization. Despite not being motivated to become an Eagle Scout (I made it as far as Life Scout), I absolutely loved camping. Luckily my troop was very active, and we went out into the woods at least once a month.

Besides building fires—and what young boy doesn't love lighting things on fire?—the best part of my camping weekends had to be the amazing wilderness hikes that we took. The nice thing about campgrounds and hiking trails is that the various pathways are marked. That means that someone had to go first and blaze that trail. When those trailblazers were setting their markers, they had to make decisions about how to navigate around natural obstacles. The best of them deliberately created a path to maximize the experience of natural beauty.

The same holds true when we create discipleship pathways in our strategic pastoral plans. These pathways arise out of the choices we make as a community regarding what we offer and how we accompany others on this journey toward Christ. As we once again contemplate our formula for change (D x V x F>R), where D = dissatisfaction with current state, V = vision of the future, F = first concrete steps to get there, and R = resistance to change, it becomes clear that in order to invest F (first concrete steps to get there) with the most value, thereby increasing our chances that we will overcome the resistance (R), we need to create strategic pastoral plans that acknowledge our current reality. These plans must describe in easy-to-understand terms how we move from current state to future state. The more focused we are on these discipleship pathways, the more fruit our plans will bear.

In order to help dioceses and parishes develop strategic pastoral plans that incarnate the five paradigm shifts, we have created a process we call Take a Leap into Cultural Change. Note that we designed this process specifically for parishes and dioceses whose leaders were feeling overwhelmed, didn't know where to start, or didn't have experience or skills in strategic planning. Nevertheless, all those we have accompanied have found that this process helped them in their efforts to create strategic pastoral plans that bear fruit.

Take a Leap

To borrow the old adage, a journey of a thousand miles begins with the first step. You've covered your community with prayer, motivated the dissatisfied to come on a journey, discovered what that journey will be and where it will lead (missioning and visioning)—now you are ready to take the leap and start planning. But where do you start?

Taking the First Steps (Pastoral Planning)

Step 1: Take a Cultural Snapshot

In order to figure out how to get where we want to go, we need to know where we are. There are some good tools that parishes can use to discover what their current culture is.

The Gallup organization has developed a survey—ME 25—designed to measure engagement. (Remember, though, that Gallup defines engagement much more broadly than we do in our paradigm of engagement: engagement in our paradigm is primarily about attendance and doing things.) The ME 25 assesses the engagement levels of a community's members by examining twenty-five (thus its name) key indicators of engagement. The survey is a result of Gallup's social scientists' research involving decades of data surrounding this topic.

To use this tool well requires a commitment of time and money, as well as the willingness to examine where your particular parish sits relative to others in regard to member engagement. When used well, the survey can help you create clear and fruitful strategic pastoral plans.

In my travels to speak at conferences, as well as in my direct accompaniment of parishes and dioceses, it became clear to me that many parishes weren't ready to make the investment required by the ME 25 Survey. So I created a simple-to-use qualitative tool, aptly named the Cultural Snapshot Inventory (CSI), designed to foster conversation and assessment of the current state of parishes and dioceses relative to the five paradigm shifts we have been discussing. Gather your various leaders, and have them go through the inventory.

You can find a copy of the CSI in appendix C of this book. Free copies of this inventory can be downloaded from the M3 Ministries website, at http://m3catholic.com/csi.

Note: The following steps assume that teams will only be addressing one paradigm of their choosing at a time, but you could decide to work on all five paradigms at once. If your parish leadership has been overwhelmed, however, and you don't have a lot of experience creating plans, we don't recommend tackling all five at once. If you do have the skills, resources, and desire to work on all five, you can do so by making adjustments for time and resources as you go along. Eventually your teams should cover all five paradigm shifts as you formulate your strategic plan.

Step 2: Discuss

The next step in the Take a Leap process involves discussion. The CSI will give you a score detailing how well your parish is doing in relation to each of the five paradigm shifts, but there's more to the inventory than that. Its purpose is to foster discussion, create a sense of urgency around cultural change, promote unity, and identify potential obstacles and resources that will hinder or help transformation. Therefore, after your leadership has taken the inventory, bring your teams together, and then choose one of the five paradigm shifts for discussion. Specific discussion questions around each of the paradigms are in appendix D of this book.

Step 3: Pray

In addition to grounding the larger three-phase approach to parish renewal in intercessory prayer, the third step in the Take a Leap process also involves prayer. The key decision makers—those individuals who will help create the actual strategic pastoral plan—will now take time to pray over all the feedback they received in step two of this process. This period of prayer should take place anywhere between a few days and up to four weeks after step two is completed. The focus should be on asking the Lord to help the team discern the next steps to take in order for the community to experience renewal and transformation.

Step 4: Discern Leverage Points

In the fourth step, those leaders responsible for creating a strategic pastoral plan should meet, and focusing on the paradigm shift they've been praying about, each team member should share the fruit of their prayer and discernment, listing

- one concrete thing the parish or diocese could do in the next week to foster a shift to the new paradigm;
- one concrete thing the parish or diocese could do in the next six months to foster a shift to that paradigm; and
- one concrete thing the parish or diocese could do in the next year to foster a shift to that paradigm.

Similarly, each person should bring to the table a list of what the parish should *stop* doing in the next week, six months, and year in order to facilitate a shift to that particular paradigm. These ideas should, of course, build off of the parish's vision, mission, and values.

Here's what that might look like. Let's say your team has been tasked with creating the strategic pastoral plan and you decide as a team to focus on the shift from engagement to encounter. Each of you has spent two weeks in prayer asking the Lord to show you what that might look like for your community. Each of you has also sifted through the feedback offered by the larger initial group that met to discuss the Cultural Snapshot Inventory in step two; you've taken that to prayer as well. Now, as you begin step four, you each come to the team meeting with three suggestions that you believe will help foster a shift from engagement to encounter in your parish. When it is your turn in that meeting, you might say the following:

- In the next week, we can ask our parish greeters to come a few minutes early and pray together that God might use them as channels of his love as they welcome people who come to the parish church for Sunday Mass.
- In the next six months, we can revamp our parish registration process to make it more prayerful, personal, and rooted in love. When people ask us about parish registration, or when they come to register, our goal is to make them feel welcomed and to find out how we can serve and accompany them. In that way, our registration process can more directly help others encounter Jesus.
- In the next year, we can launch the Alpha Course at our parish as a way of helping members of our community and the unchurched fall in love with Jesus.

Each of the other team members will present their lists as well.

Step 5: Make a Plan

At this point, the team members crafting the game plan should discuss which of the proposed changes in the short, medium, and long term will yield the greatest fruit *for the particular paradigm on which they are focused.* Then they should further discern—following more prayer and an assessment of the resources available to their parish—which of these changes their community will focus on during the next twelve months. These changes might contain a mix of short-term (in the next week) and mid- to long-term (six months to a year) initiatives.

Once the team has decided on these initiatives, they should put together the plan details. These will include the steps required to introduce the initiative into the life of the community; the dates by which each step of the initiative must be completed; the names of whoever is responsible for finishing those steps; and the completion date. In addition, one person should be designated as project coordinator, responsible for following up with all involved to make sure that the work is being done as planned and on time. These initiative coordinators will update the senior leadership team regularly regarding the progress of an initiative. Ideally, these coordinators would be proactive, able to signal ahead of time if, for example, the initiative is going to miss a critical date.

In the end, the senior leadership team, or whoever is responsible for crafting the strategic pastoral plan, including the pastor, must hold each other accountable for the successful coordination and execution of each initiative. They should also make sure they have a communication plan in place to help the community understand the who, what, where, when, and why of these initiatives.

Step 6: Take Action

Don't let fear of any kind stop you from taking the final step in the Take a Leap process. You have to take action. Once you decide on your initiatives, create a project plan, assign coordinators, and begin building your communications plan, you have to actually start doing it. Again, regular updates here are exceptionally important, as is being willing to hold each other accountable.

Note that taking action will require more communication and more meetings for the team members tasked with creating the plan—and this might run afoul of Catholic parish culture. Typically our major committees and councils meet monthly, and the terms for the folks on those teams are generally three years. That means that an average leadership team—the finance council, parish council, social justice committee, for example—has twelve meetings a year for three years.

But things are different in the real world. Let's drill down and do the math. On paper, we're looking at a total of thirty-six meetings for these committees, each one lasting about two hours, for a total of seventy-two hours of meetings spread over three years. You and I know, however, that nothing really gets done during December meetings—those are mostly Christmas parties—or January meetings, when people are still recovering from the holidays. In addition, it seems as if the Holy Spirit takes the summers off from many Catholic parishes—often teams don't meet during June, July, and August!

If you've been following along, this means that, on a practical level, the number of monthly meetings can fall to as few as seven per year for a total of twenty-one meetings over three years.

If each of those lasted two hours, we are now talking about a total of forty-two hours over three years in which to move the needle on parish transformation. Needless to say, our leadership teams will have to meet more frequently and become much more focused if we want to experience the renewal God desires for us.

Results

As you can see, there is nothing mysterious or magical about the Take a Leap process. It is a simple approach that uses common-sense principles and an understanding of the five essential paradigm shifts to help leaders at the parish and diocesan levels approach their community's life differently. And yet I have witnessed time and time again that this bare-bones approach can unlock a leadership team that has felt stuck for a long time and give staff, key volunteers, and other parish leaders a common language around which to rally.

Here's how Samantha Denefe, director of evangelization and faith formation for Our Lady of the Holy Souls Parish in the Diocese of Little Rock, explains her community's experience using the Take a Leap process and the Cultural Snapshot Inventory:

> At my parish we started focusing on intentional discipleship and parish renewal in 2015. The whole staff read *Forming Intentional Disciples*. The first phase was to renew our parishioners who were already hungry. To do this we partnered with The Evangelical Catholic to implement evangelizing small groups. After our three-year alliance with EC ended, we had a strong base of intentional disciples. At that point, we knew it was important

to bring together our parish leadership with those disciples we had produced.

We launched a monthly program and invited anyone in leadership. We knew we were ready to start trying to change the culture on a wider level. However, we struggled through different homegrown materials for about a year, and nothing really changed. I wanted something that could clearly communicate what I had come to know through all my research and life experience with the new evangelization and its focus on intentional discipleship, but I couldn't find anything!

Until we discovered the Cultural Snapshot Inventory.

Our pastor took the inventory to a priests' continuing-education day. Then he brought it back for the staff to look at. We went through the inventory and had some great conversations, which opened our eyes to the value of that tool. We believed it was something that could help us change the culture of our parish! We had struck gold!

We decided to spend six months working through the Cultural Inventory Snapshot with our leadership. Although the inventory was difficult for many of them, they found the questions themselves to be formative. After that, we met several times each month and followed the Take a Leap process as we worked our way through each of the five paradigm shifts.

These tools clearly defined where we were and where we wanted to be. With that knowledge, we have seen amazing fruits through a shift in our leadership. There is a camaraderie and unity as we have banded together under the goal of creating a culture that fosters intentional discipleship. I have no doubt that this unity comes from having hard and honest conversations sparked by the inventory about the needs of the parishioners. And as needs have been identified, leadership has stepped up, feeling called by God to answer those needs. Perhaps the most amazing thing of all is that this process has created an environment where we pursue change together rather than just dismissing it out of hand. Our people are hungry to create a culture of intentional discipleship.

It has been, and still will be, a difficult journey. We haven't completely shifted paradigms yet, but we can see it coming. We are in the "transition" zone on each of the five paradigm shifts. And that is an exciting place to be in parish renewal!

Samantha and her parish have spent time aligning around a clear vision and mission. The Take a Leap process has helped prepare leadership to create a strategic pastoral plan that intentionally operationalizes (or integrates) the five paradigm shifts into the life and organization of the community. They are still in the very early stages of taking the first steps, and only time will tell what fruit emerges from this community. However, their ability to walk this path is significantly strengthened by their common language and direction, as well as the growing fellowship they are experiencing as a community of leaders.

ABLAZE

You can download a free overview of the Take a Leap Process, which includes the Five Paradigm Shift Discussion Questions, by going to http://m3catholic.com/take-a-leap.

12

Power for Change

I want to share with you a story that I heard several years ago.

Once upon a time, there was a company that experienced tremendous growth. No matter how much they tried to staff up to meet the demands of the market, they just couldn't keep up. As a result, one department in particular had to work exceptionally hard. None of the employees in that department could ever take any vacation time. Thus the members of that department were always looking for ways to get a break.

One day two employees were working side by side at their desks, when the first employee said to the second, "I know how we are going to get some time off."

The second employee turned to the first and said, "How?"

"Just watch me, and follow my lead," said the first employee.

Immediately the first employee climbed up on his desk and began removing the ceiling tiles right above him, exposing a series of pipes. Without hesitation he climbed up onto the pipes and, wrapping his legs tightly around them, hung upside down over his desk. A few minutes later, his manager came walking out of her office and, upon seeing the employee hanging upside down, blurted out, "What do you think you're doing?"

"I'm a light bulb," replied the employee. "I bring light to this whole office."

"Well, I think you're crazy," his manager retorted. "And I need you to come down from there right now, get your things, and

ABLAZE

leave. I don't want to see you back in the office again, until you have a note from your psychologist that you are better."

Dutifully the first employee climbed down from his perch, logged off his computer, and headed out the door. Seeing this, the second employee logged off his computer and started walking toward the door as well.

His manager, catching sight of him, yelled, "And where do you think you're going?"

"Home," the second employee replied. "I can't work in the dark!"

I often use this story during parish missions to drive home a point. The first employee in this little tale is acting in a way that is inconsistent with his fundamental identity. Obviously he is not a light bulb! Just so, we as the Church act in a way that is inconsistent with our identity, not only in our personal walk with Jesus but also in the communal dimensions of our life.

I'm not just talking about sin. Sometimes we lose sight of who we are. What do I mean?

The Church is more than a sociological collection of people who all believe the same thing and seek to advance the cause of Christ. Nor are we simply a human organization. The Church is the body of the risen Jesus alive and at work in the world today. In all this talk of paradigms, multi-phase approaches to cultural change, and strategic pastoral planning, it's easy to lose sight of a fundamental reality: life in Christ is, at heart, grounded in the supernatural and oriented toward eternity. This supernatural life may bring the natural to perfection, but it is not limited to the natural.

Remember the secret sauce of the Divine Renovation approach? The best of human organizational principles, coupled with a deep understanding of evangelization and an intentional cooperation with the supernatural dimensions of life in Christ. We have more at our disposal than organizational dynamics, tools for cultural change, and leadership development processes. We have the power of the kingdom, which God has released in us through his Son Jesus, in the Holy Spirit.

Too often, however, we suffer from what I call *pneumaphobia*—fear of the Holy Spirit. We're excited when the Solemnity of Pentecost rolls around each year. The altar linens are red, the liturgical vestments are red, and people in the assembly often wear red shirts. We congratulate each other and say, "Happy Birthday," to the Church. And then when Pentecost is over, we put the Holy Spirit back in the Holy Spirit box.

Until Confirmation. At that time, we get excited again. The bishop's coming! There are banners all over the Church with flaming doves and tongues of fire. The sacred oils are out, and we say, "Yay, Holy Spirit." And then when the celebration of Confirmation is over, we put the Holy Spirit back in the Holy Spirit box, and we ask him not to bother us again until next year—because frankly, we find the Holy Spirit and the mystery of his activity unsettling.

As Fr. James Mallon has said, many Christians "may have heard that there is a Holy Spirit, but have virtually no experience of the Holy Spirit and no relationship with the Spirit of Power."[44]

That's why the path of parish and diocesan renewal requires both personal and pastoral conversion. We must allow the power of God to change and transform us, so that we can more authentically live our individual and communal identities in Christ. As I wrote in my book *The 10 Biggest Lies of the Enemy—And How to Combat Them*,

> Wherever Jesus went in his earthly ministry, he changed hearts and transformed lives, releasing the power of his kingdom—and he still does. Those who have received the indwelling of the Holy Spirit at Baptism *are already walking in the reality of God's kingdom and his power.*[45]

He fills us with the presence and power of the kingdom, so that we might become more like Jesus—not just for ourselves but for the sake of all those we meet in this life.

There can be no parish or diocesan renewal without a deliberate cooperation with the person, presence, and power of the Holy Spirit. We must embrace an attitude of *pneumaphilia*—love of the Holy Spirit—which welcomes, invites, and leaves a privileged place for the Holy Spirit in our personal lives and in our parish and diocesan communities. When we prioritize the reality of kingdom life—life in the Spirit—amazing breakthroughs happen.

In the course of my ministry, I have seen God work through natural *and* supernatural means to bring healing, forgiveness, and transformation where it might not otherwise have happened. It is not unusual in the course of parish missions, workshops, and conferences for people to experience physical, spiritual, and emotional healing—*often when we aren't even specifically praying for those things.*

If all of that seems a little too "out there" for us, then perhaps we have become unmoored from our deepest identity as members of Christ's body. We should ask ourselves why we are willing to believe that bread becomes the Lord of the universe at every validly celebrated Mass but have a difficult time believing that God wants to work through us—the children for whom he has poured out his life—in supernatural ways.

We can no longer afford, as parishes and dioceses, to operate solely out of our human talents and resources. Principles of organizational change, processes for leading change, strategic plans, solid efforts in financial development—these will never be enough, on their own, to invigorate, renew, and restore life to the Church. We need the Holy Spirit!

All of these principles, processes and plan can, however, work together so that a more positive disposition to the supernatural dimensions of kingdom life can take root in our communities. Thus our parishes and dioceses will become not only places filled with life for the Catholic community but also life-giving outposts of the kingdom, where the Father's heart is made known to *all* his children. My deepest hope and prayer is that this simple book can bless the parishes and dioceses filled with God's people and help them bear the kind of fruit that will last.

To God be the glory!

APPENDIX A
Six Disciplines of Discipleship[46]

"Whoever wishes to come after me must deny himself,
take up his cross, and follow me."
—Matthew 16:24

When Jesus called the Twelve Apostles, he invited each of them to follow him, and that call is extended to every human person. The words that Jesus uses to call us are active, not passive . . . If we want to live as disciples we must "deny," "take up," and "follow." There is an intentionality to discipleship. One doesn't become a disciple simply by birth, or cultural affiliation, or profession. We aren't necessarily disciples because we were born into a Catholic family, or because we are Irish (or other ethnicity), or even because we work for the Church. Discipleship emerges out of a sustained encounter with the Lord in the midst of his Church and a conscious decision to choose Christ each day.

Sherry Weddell, in her landmark book *Forming Intentional Disciples,* writes on how we become disciples:

> By acting like Simon Peter: "Jesus said to Simon, 'Do not be afraid; henceforth you will be catching men.' And when they had brought their boats to land, they left everything and followed him." (Luke 5:10-11)

Simon's experience was not exceptional, either in human terms or in the tradition of the Church. No one voluntarily sheds his or her job, home, and whole way of life accidentally or unconsciously. Simon Peter's "drop the net decision" is what we mean by disciple. From the moment he dropped his nets to follow Jesus, he was a disciple.[47]

The Great Story of Jesus, although it has cosmic dimensions, penetrates into the personal—into the heart of every man, woman, and child with ears to hear. When we respond with an openness of heart—when we say yes to what the Great Story, and the One who is at the center of that story, offers us—the path of discipleship opens up to us.

The word "disciple" comes from the Latin *discipulus* and it means "one who learns." In the culture of Jesus' time, a disciple sat at the foot of a rabbi (teacher) and learned from him. Disciples were expected to take on the lifestyle of the one they followed, absorbing not only knowledge but their rabbi's way of life. In his interactions both with the original twelve disciples and now with each of us, Jesus keeps this dimension of discipleship and goes a step further. Jesus doesn't simply want his disciples to act like him; rather we are invited to become like him. We do this through the outpouring of his life, which comes to us through the power of the Holy Spirit.

Christian disciples then are men and women who have heard the Great Story of Jesus, who have allowed it to penetrate and enter the circumstances of their lives, and who have given themselves over to Jesus. In this way, they bear that story (and the one who sits at its center) within them and become heralds of it to everyone they meet. St. Paul talks about this in a related way when he writes that "we are ambassadors for Christ, as if God were appealing through us" (2 Corinthians 5:20). The power of the Great Story is the reality of the kingdom lived out in the daily rhythms of life.

What Does Discipleship Look Like?

Although the working of God's grace on each human heart is a mystery, and each person responds uniquely to God's invitation to relationship, discipleship looks like something. Though each person's discipleship is uniquely lived out, all disciples share some common characteristics. For example, since discipleship is an intentional choice to enter into a relationship with Jesus in the midst of his Church, someone who is a disciple can articulate (even at the most basic level) their own experience of that relationship, what it is like to be in a loving relationship with Jesus.

In a similar way, all mature disciples of Jesus embrace six common disciplines—habits of life that are both expressions of their love for Jesus and ways that they grow in union with him. So what are the disciplines of discipleship? While a full exploration of each of these disciplines is worthy of a book, here's a quick summary:

Daily Scripture Reading

The Bible is the very word of God and, along with the teaching of the apostles, makes up the foundation of the Christian faith. The author of the Book of Hebrews had this to say about the power of the word of God: "Indeed, the word of God is living and effective, sharper than any two-edged sword, penetrating even between soul and spirit, joints and marrow, and able to discern reflections and thoughts of the heart" (Hebrews 4:12). Through the power of the Holy Spirit, we encounter the risen and living Jesus in a personal way when we read the Scriptures. God's desire is to meet us, speak to us, instruct us, console us, and challenge and transform us in and through our reading of Scripture *every single day*.

If you grew up Catholic, you may have the sense that someone told you not to read the Bible or discouraged you from picking it up. Or you may have had a very large, coffee-table Bible in your home that seemed too ornamental or unwieldy to sit and read. Or perhaps the Bible just seems too difficult to understand, and that makes you uncomfortable to try it.

The reality is that the Bible is accessible, and reading it is an essential part of being a disciple. If you are not sure how to start reading the Bible, then I suggest beginning with the Gospel of Mark in the New Testament. It is the shortest of the four gospels, and you can take fifteen minutes each day and read just one chapter a day, asking the Lord to open your heart to his voice before you read it.

It is important to read Scripture with "the mind of the Church," meaning that we read the Bible connected to the Church's teaching authority. It is equally important to read Scripture with "the ears of the heart," in order to begin to discern the voice of God as he speaks to us through his word. This is more than simply learning the Scriptures through participating in a Bible study (though taking advantage of Bible study groups can be very important as you grow in Christ). It means reading with a prayerful attitude of receptivity, listening with the ears of your heart for whatever God wants to say to you specifically.

Daily Prayer

At the heart of the kingdom is relationship—intimacy, encounter, and communion. Jesus lived that out on earth through his daily times of prayer. Prayer unites our heart with God's heart, allowing us to spend time with the one whom we are growing to love more deeply.

Before I married my wife, we spent time together, getting to know one another and growing in intimacy. Prayer is simply getting to know God. It can come in many forms. There are standard rote prayers that we say (the Our Father and the Hail Mary, for example). There are devotions (like the Rosary and the Stations of the Cross). There are more formal liturgical prayers (like the Mass and the Divine Office). Prayer can occur anywhere and at any time throughout the day. What it requires is some focused time with the Lord.

In prayer we engage in a dialogue with the Lord. While it is important that we speak to the Lord what is on our hearts, it is also critical that we learn how to hear his response. There are many books and resources on prayer, but there is no substitute for being personally formed by someone who understands this discipline. Your pastor, another priest, a deacon, or another member of your parish's staff can be a great resource in teaching you how to pray.

Living a Sacramental Life

The sacraments are particular and effective encounters with Jesus Christ. When we participate in and celebrate the sacraments, we receive an outpouring of God's life that changes us, helping us become holy and more like Christ. A disciple lives a conscious sacramental life, which means regular weekly (and sometimes daily) attendance at Mass, as well as frequent reception of the Sacrament of Reconciliation. Simply put, a disciple does not stay away from the sacraments.

If it has been a while since you went to Mass or Confession, I want to encourage you to return. Discipleship is an experience of kingdom life, of communion and relationship with God. Our sin and brokenness can interfere with that relationship. In his goodness, God pours out more of his life for us in the sacraments, so we can be restored. When we fall in our journey with Christ, there is no condemnation. Instead the Father invites us to receive his mercy again and again in the sacraments. With his grace, we are restored. He lifts us up and sets us on the path again—and we receive his power to deal with the temptations and obstacles we encounter.

Fellowship

Membership in the Church is not like membership in a club or a nonprofit, volunteer, or civic organization. The baptized are incorporated into Christ's body and share a bond that goes far deeper than even the natural bond that joins the human race together. The experience of life in the kingdom is not solitary but communal, characterized by mutuality and interdependence. Communion with God, by definition, includes communion with all who are in relationship with him.

Thus the call to relationship with Christ as a disciple is a call into community and deep fellowship. Because of Christ, our lives no longer make any sense apart from each other. Therefore, as baptized brothers and sisters in the Lord, we must live out this fellowship in community, provide support for each other, and even go out and serve the world together. I like to say that Christians are like charcoal briquettes—we burn hotter, brighter, and longer when we remain connected to each other.

This kind of fellowship goes beyond coffee and donuts after Mass or participation in the occasional pancake breakfast. This kind of fellowship with each other is a sharing of our life in Christ together. One of the most powerful expressions of fellowship can be found in what are called small faith communities or Christian small groups. These are small gatherings of Christians, usually in a home or at the parish, who get together to pray, learn, laugh, and support each other. I strongly encourage you to find one of these groups and join—or start one of your own!

Service

Disciples must live out the radical self-offering of Jesus by offering our very selves for the sake of the world—especially for the poor and suffering. This is not simply out of altruism, volunteerism, or on ethical and moral grounds but foundationally, because we know that Christ is present in each human person and God holds a special place in his heart for those who are poor and suffering.

The call to service is found in one of the most recognizable passages in the New Testament, John 3:16—"For God so loved the world that he gave his only Son, so that everyone who believes in him might not perish but might have eternal life." God's love for the world was so great that he *gave*. If we then profess to follow him and hold his life within us, how can we not give for the sake of others?

This kind of giving includes acts of charity and mercy, but it also encompasses applying gospel values to issues of injustice in the world today. Where are those issues in your local community or neighborhood? Where is Christ present to you in the poor and the unwanted? How can you bring the power of the kingdom to bear for the person in need whom you encounter?

Evangelizing (Sharing Christ with Others)

The heart of the Church's mission is to share Christ with others, to make Christ present in word and deed so the kingdom of God manifests powerfully in the world. When we encounter Christ, we encounter the one for whom our hearts were made, and we discover who we are, our purpose, and our destiny. This is an experience the Lord wants all of his children to have, not a special few.

At some point, as kingdom life takes a hold of you, your life will begin to change—and people will notice. When they ask questions, when they want to know what has happened to you, tell them! You don't need a theology degree or advanced training. If you are excited about what you believe and what that belief has done for your life, then talk about it.

At its most basic, evangelization is helping others encounter the Jesus to whom we have given ourselves. Disciples spend time intentionally sharing the love of the Father with others in word and deed!

If we want to help our people move from a paradigm of institutional faith to intentional faith, and if we want to set the stage for a radical missionary response from our parishioners—a movement from a maintenance paradigm to a missionary paradigm—then we have to provide continuing formation oriented toward maturing disciples in each of these six disciplines.

APPENDIX B
Seven Qualities of Fruitful Pastoral Leaders

If evangelization and accompaniment are the core components of the engine that drives parish renewal, leadership is the essential fluid that cools and lubricates that engine, allowing every component to perform at maximum efficiency. Without authentic leadership, the engine of cultural change fails to start, or overheats, or blows a gasket, coming to a complete stop.

If we are going to take the New Evangelization seriously and truly live out the Church's mission, we need to form, raise up, hire, and nurture authentic pastoral leaders who can bear great fruit. The hard truth is that many of our parishes are not led well, and the blame isn't simply on the pastors, priests, and deacons. Our entire leadership culture often suppresses innovation, uses intimidation and manipulation masked in pious language, promotes mediocrity, and is more concerned with external data (numbers of people who go through our programs and processes) than spiritual fruitfulness. Often our parishes live, lead, and struggle out of silos rather than focused and generous collaboration.

The context of our current crisis only highlights the dire necessity of leadership transformation. There are no other options: we either embrace a fundamental change in how we govern and live out our common baptismal life as parishes, or we just accept the fact that our future fate will be one of decline, retrenchment, and a growing irrelevance to the secular world.

Responsibility for such a change in leadership begins, first and foremost, with each of us. To that end, we at M3 Ministries have identified seven qualities of fruitful pastoral leaders to help individuals and groups of parish leaders begin this journey. In addition, we have also created a free, downloadable Leadership Resource to assist you. You can download the free resource by going to **http://m3catholic.com/seven-qualities.**

Note: We chose to use the word "fruitful" rather than "effective" *to highlight an important reality*: leadership isn't simply about being able to handle the job; it's about individual and communal impact. Fruitful leaders not only change culture; they change people. In addition, each of these seven qualities rests on the foundation of vision. Not every leader in your parish has the ability to see, articulate, and promote a *new vision, but all leaders* must internalize the vision of the community and live it out in such a way that others are drawn in.

The Seven Qualities Revealed

Discipled: First and foremost, a fruitful pastoral leader must be a disciple—one who has had an encounter with Jesus and chooses to follow him in the midst of his Church. The discipleship process cannot be understood "from the outside." Fruitful pastoral leaders understand the spiritual journey toward discipleship and know how to help others entrust their lives to Jesus.

Invested: Effective pastoral leaders invest in the mission of the community or organization. They are present and proactive in the process of helping their community live out that mission. In addition to this "mission alignment," authentic leaders invest in the people they serve, seeking to build them up—even when it isn't convenient.

Relational: Fruitful pastoral leaders understand that, ultimately, their role is to foster their own relationship with Jesus as well as the relationship of others with Jesus, and they create cultures that prioritize those relationships. One of the key ways they do this is by accompanying others relationally. Even if their role has a large administrative component, they never lose sight of the reality that it is all about Jesus and the people they serve. This extends to their colleagues and other staff members. Effective pastoral leaders build a web of authentic relationships and choose to work collaboratively rather than in silos.

Accountable: Pastoral leaders who bear sustained fruit in their ministry prioritize accountability. They hold themselves responsible for delivering on their objectives and expect others to do so too. Working in teams, these leaders do not hesitate to hold their team members accountable. When difficulties arise, they do not scapegoat or shift blame; they step up, take responsibility, and look for solutions. Accountable pastoral leaders do not hesitate to have difficult conversations with team members, peers, and their own leaders, to bring clarity, reinforce healthy boundaries, and address issues.

Discerning: In order to bear the most fruit, effective pastoral leaders discern the direction and will of God for themselves, their community, their ministry, and the people they serve. This begins with prayer and attentiveness to the movement of God, coupled with a growing detachment from their own plans and visions. Discerning leaders prioritize prayer as a leadership team and seek the will of God together.

Surrendered: Effective pastoral leadership begins with the deep understanding that nothing can truly grow and move forward by our own power; all depends upon the power and presence of God. Fruitful leaders invite the Holy Spirit to move in their ministries, expect that he will show up, and leave room for his direction and action.

Empowering: Fruitful pastoral leaders know that they do not have all the gifts necessary to move and transform a community or organization. Therefore they seek out, nurture, and support others. These leaders are not threatened by the giftedness of others—even when these gifts exist to a greater degree than their own—and they actively work to help others grow into leadership roles.

For Reflection

The work of raising up a generation of fruitful pastoral leaders begins with us. Therefore it is important that we take an honest look at our own development as ministers and leaders in a pastoral context. Spend some time prayerfully reviewing the following reflection questions. You might find it useful to return to these questions on a regular basis.

1. How would I rate myself in terms of each of the seven qualities? In what quality am I the strongest? Where am I in most need of improvement?

2. Which people in my life can I ask to give me an honest and forthright assessment of my development in each of the seven qualities? Whom can I ask to hold me accountable to that development?

3. When I think about "acting out of" or "growing in" these seven qualities, do any make me nervous or uncomfortable? Why?

4. What do I perceive is the biggest obstacle that keeps me from growing in any of the seven qualities? What resources or assistance will I need in overcoming those obstacles?

5. Given my current pastoral situation, which of the seven qualities do I need most? What is one thing I can commit to in the next week in order to grow in that quality? What is one thing I can commit to over the next six months so that I can grow in that quality?

APPENDIX C
The Cultural Snapshot Inventory

In order to help parishes clarify their current culture relative to the five paradigms, we at M3 Ministries have created a simple-to-use Cultural Snapshot Inventory. Originally designed for use by staff and the people who work most closely with them, it can also be used by pastoral and finance council members, leaders of specific ministries, and key volunteers. We direct those individuals to take the inventory based on their own perspective. So, for example, anytime a head of ministry or key volunteer comes across a reference to staff in the inventory or a question about the whole community that they don't have enough experience, exposure, or data to answer, we encourage them to answer in terms of their specific area of ministry.

Rather than providing an objective, scientific analysis of a parish's culture, the purpose of this inventory is to create a starting point for a leadership group as they begin to walk the path of cultural change. In many respects, the journey through the inventory is more important than the snapshot produced at the end. The point is to start discussion, dialogue, and sharing that will lead to a transition to the new paradigms—both in parish leaders and in the community as a whole. Used in conjunction with the streamlined process for cultural change outlined in chapter 10, the inventory can be a powerful tool that helps parish leaders move from a place of overwhelmed paralysis to substantive cultural change.

ABLAZE

M3 Ministries has created free downloadable copies of the inventory for your use. Simply go to **http://m3catholic.com/csi,** and download those files if you don't want to mark up your book.

Cultural Snapshot Inventory

The following inventory is a tool to help you get a better sense of where your parish is culturally relative to the five paradigm shifts. Read each statement carefully, and indicate to what degree it is true for your parish *at the present time,* using the following scale:

0—not true at all; 1—somewhat true; 2—mostly true; 3—definitely true

1. We take time as a staff to pray together regularly (beyond just starting meetings with a brief prayer).

2. We have a clearly defined discernment process in place to help us match volunteers with the appropriate ministry.

3. Many parishioners understand that their Baptism configures them in a particular way for service to the world, and they are open and excited about serving.

4. We use "off-the-shelf" programs and processes (for example, Ascension Press Bible studies or *Be My Witness* from Renew International) as part of a defined strategy to help people move from unchurched or culturally Catholic to missionary disciples.

5. Our parish leadership strives to listen when disagreements arise and to act compassionately and professionally toward the individual or group who disagrees with them. They are quick to apologize when they don't act professionally, even if they stick with their original strategy or decision.

6. Most members of our parish understand and agree that being Catholic involves an intimate, personal relationship with Jesus Christ in the midst of his Church.

7. We design and sponsor events throughout the year that help people encounter the person of Jesus Christ. These are not primarily offered as adult enrichment or even as catechetical events but as opportunities to encounter Jesus.

8. We spend at least as much money on initiatives that focus on the community outside the parish as we do on initiatives that focus on the parish community.

9. It is a good thing to have intentional disciples in our staff positions—including administrative and support roles.

10. We clearly define performance expectations and "scope of role" for staff members, key leaders, and volunteers.

11. As a whole, members of our community readily talk to one another about their relationship with Christ.

12. People have regular opportunities to encounter and wrestle with the kerygma (the Good News of Jesus Christ) as they experience parish life.

13. Most parishioners can make an explicit connection between their acts of service in the world (charity and justice, for example) and the Good News of Jesus Christ

14. We regularly offer formation that equips parishioners to accompany others on the journey into discipleship.

15. Lack of fruit, poor performance, personal issues, and professional difficulties are dealt with quickly, clearly, and compassionately.

16. The work of pastoral staff members and key leaders in our parish is evaluated based on their fruitfulness in helping others become disciples, mature as disciples, and go out on mission.

17. Taking the time to make sure we have the right person with the right gifts in a particular area of service or ministry (for example, a catechist) is more important than filling that position as fast as possible.

18. Our parish has a firm grasp on the major issues of our local civic community and is explicitly working as a faith community on addressing those issues.

19. We specifically choose disciples, particularly those who have been equipped to accompany others, as small group leaders for our programs and processes.

20. There is a high degree of trust among staff, council, commission, and committee members at the parish.

21. We regularly offer opportunities for people to explicitly commit themselves to Christ as his disciples.

22. We have examined the major facets of parish life to see how they foster an encounter with the person of Jesus Christ.

23. Our major focus is on forming individuals to discover their gifts and discern their call in the world, rather than on preparing individuals to take on leadership roles within the parish.

24. Many parishioners understand the Great Story of Salvation (the kerygma), know how their story and the Great Story intersect, and can communicate that clearly to others.

25. Passive-aggressive behavior is brought into the light and addressed in a professional manner.

26. In general, our parishioners are comfortable praying with and for one another, using their own words rather than always using formal prayers.

27. We have changed structures, processes, and events in the parish so that they more readily help others encounter Jesus.

28. We actively discourage people from spending too much of their time working inside—within the parish, on initiatives, ministries, and committees—rather than in the world (which is the primary vocation of lay men and women).

29. It is normal for our parish to provide follow-up after a program ends to see how that particular program may have moved participants along in their spiritual journey.

30. We do not avoid conflict when it arises or let it fester and grow, but rather we deal with it immediately or as soon as is proper to do so—and this is modeled particularly by our pastor.

31. We have a clear pathway for the unchurched to become disciples, grow as disciples, and be equipped as missionary disciples.

32. If the right leader doesn't emerge for a new or important initiative, we pray, communicate our need, and then wait until the right leader steps up before moving forward with the initiative.

33. Our primary focus is on helping people commit their lives entirely to Jesus and living out that commitment daily, rather than on soliciting commitments of time, talent, and treasure from our members.

34. We have a process that welcomes newly registered parishioners and helps them build relationships with disciples in the parish, so that new members can deepen their relationship with Christ.

35. If we have the appropriate mandate, then as staff members, leaders, or key volunteers, we are comfortable disagreeing with and even challenging our pastor or priests when discussing things like pastoral strategy, operations, and people.

36. Having a relationship with Jesus is so important that it factors into our parish's hiring decisions at all levels.

37. We see those involved in ministry as more than volunteers, and we both expect more from them and help them see themselves as channels of the Father's love in Jesus Christ.

38. We avoid using insider language (that is, language that non-Catholics, non-Christians, or strangers to the parish campus wouldn't understand) in our marketing, communication, and conversations with others.

39. We regularly have conversations with staff members, leaders, and key volunteers to get a better sense of where they are in their spiritual journey. These conversations factor into our hiring and ministry placement decisions, as well as into the support we offer these individuals.

40. In staff, council, and committee meetings, we feel comfortable having honest and even heated debate about ideas and strategies, knowing that none of the participants will interpret disagreement as a personal attack on them.

41. As we prepare people to receive particular sacraments, we explicitly invite them to commit or recommit their lives to Jesus Christ.

42. Getting people involved in the life of the parish is one part of a larger process aimed at helping people encounter Jesus.

43. We judge the vitality of our parish not so much on "counts"— for example, the number of people enrolled in religious education or attending Bible studies—but on how many we send, that is the number of missionary disciples in our community bearing fruit in the world.

44. People who come to the parish with questions about the Catholic faith or a relationship with God can easily find someone to walk with them through their questions, and it doesn't have to be a staff member.

45. Our pastor does not feel the need to manage the details of every initiative but rather gives clear direction to his direct reports, empowers them to make decisions, and then holds them accountable.

46. The fundamental focus of our community's life is the evangelization and formation of adults. This is where we spend the bulk of our time, money, and attention.

47. We would rather experience turnover in our parish membership because we speak explicitly about Jesus than keep everyone active and connected by remaining silent.

48. We recognize the importance of meeting people where they are and have created a number of "shallow entry points" or events that don't presume a deep knowledge of Catholicism or Christianity.

49. We believe that programs don't make disciples, people do.

50. If a pastoral strategy or decision is the right one, we are willing to move forward with it even if it means having difficult conversations or unpleasant consequences for a group or individual.

ABLAZE

CULTURAL INVENTORY ANSWER SHEET

Circle your answer to the appropriate question from the Cultural Snapshot Inventory. When you have completed this Inventory, add up all the number values **DOWN** each column and place the total in the box marked **TOTAL.**

Institutional to Intentional				Engagement to Encounter				Maintenance to Mission				Programs to People				Avoidance to Accountability			
N	S	M	D	N	S	M	D	N	S	M	D	N	S	M	D	N	S	M	D
1 0 1 2 3				**2** 0 1 2 3				**3** 0 1 2 3				**4** 0 1 2 3				**5** 0 1 2 3			
6 0 1 2 3				**7** 0 1 2 3				**8** 0 1 2 3				**9** 0 1 2 3				**10** 0 1 2 3			
11 0 1 2 3				**12** 0 1 2 3				**13** 0 1 2 3				**14** 0 1 2 3				**15** 0 1 2 3			
16 0 1 2 3				**17** 0 1 2 3				**18** 0 1 2 3				**19** 0 1 2 3				**20** 0 1 2 3			
21 0 1 2 3				**22** 0 1 2 3				**23** 0 1 2 3				**24** 0 1 2 3				**25** 0 1 2 3			
26 0 1 2 3				**27** 0 1 2 3				**28** 0 1 2 3				**29** 0 1 2 3				**30** 0 1 2 3			
31 0 1 2 3				**32** 0 1 2 3				**33** 0 1 2 3				**34** 0 1 2 3				**35** 0 1 2 3			
36 0 1 2 3				**37** 0 1 2 3				**38** 0 1 2 3				**39** 0 1 2 3				**40** 0 1 2 3			
41 0 1 2 3				**42** 0 1 2 3				**43** 0 1 2 3				**44** 0 1 2 3				**45** 0 1 2 3			
46 0 1 2 3				**47** 0 1 2 3				**48** 0 1 2 3				**49** 0 1 2 3				**50** 0 1 2 3			
TOTAL				TOTAL				TOTAL				TOTAL				TOTAL			

0 – 16   Your parish is firmly operating under a traditional paradigm in this particular area. Moving to a new paradigm will most likely take a lot of time and effort, and will cause moderate to major disruption as the community goes on this journey.

17 –24   Your parish is moving through a transition into a new paradigm in this area. You already have a good foundation off of which you can build bridges into the new paradigm. While the journey still requires intentionality, you likely have a growing group of parishioners who are either operating out of the new paradigm in this area or are open to it.

25 – 30   Your parish has made the paradigm shift in this area. Your effort now will likely focus on maintaining this cultural norm and passing it along to future generations within the parish community.

APPENDIX D
Paradigm Shift Discussion Questions

In order to facilitate a more focused conversation around the five paradigm shifts, we have created questions for small group discussion rooted in each of those paradigms, for step two of the Take a Leap process. Be sure to have each group record the key points of their conversation, so that the team responsible for creating the strategic pastoral plan can include them in their prayer and discernment. Like the Cultural Snapshot Inventory, these discussion questions are intended to foster greater reflection on each of the five essential paradigm shifts.

From Institutional Faith to Intentional Faith

1. Have we, as a leadership team and staff, committed ourselves to Christ as disciples?

2. Do we first and foremost lay a groundwork of prayer and intercession for our work together, and do we take time to pray together as a team, beyond opening and closing prayers?

3. Do we talk about, preach about, form others in, and otherwise make personal relationship with Christ (in the midst of his Church) a normal expectation and component of parish life?

4. Does the question of whether a person is an intentional disciple of Jesus Christ factor into our hiring decisions?

5. Have we taken the time to see how all of our programs, processes, and activities might lead to a game plan of discipleship or a path into missionary discipleship?

From Engagement to Encounter

1. Have we examined every facet of parish life and evaluated how well it helps others encounter Jesus?

2. Are we satisfied with "adding bodies" to our ministries that need volunteers, regardless of whether a person has the gifts to serve in those ministries?

3. If our goal is to get more people involved, what is our hope for these people, and what will we do with them once they start showing up?

4. Do we, as leaders, understand the kerygma? How do we share that Good News with others? In what ways do we help our people encounter the story of Jesus?

From Maintenance to Mission

1. Do we, as leaders, and do our people, understand that our Baptism calls us to serve the world?

2. How much of our time, energy, and money is spent on actions and activities that point inward, toward the community?

3. How comfortable are our people in sharing Jesus with others? What do we need to do to help them grow in this area?

4. What are three of the biggest issues, difficulties, or obstacles facing our parish's civic community? What are we, as a people, doing about them?

From Programs to People

1. Do we have a sense of where our staff, key leaders, and volunteers are in their individual spiritual journeys? What about our wider community?

2. Do we form our people to walk alongside others, helping parishioners learn how to encourage, instruct, and pray with those who are enquiring about or on the path to becoming disciples?

3. How do our programs directly and intentionally lead others to make a decision for Christ?

4. Have we constructed clearly linked pathways that help the unchurched encounter Christ, choose to follow him, grow as his disciples, and become equipped as missionary disciples?

ABLAZE

From Avoidance to Accountability

1. Are we, as staff and leaders, willing to have difficult but necessary conversations with each other, as well as with those we serve, when the need arises?

2. Do we offer each other feedback on how we are doing relative to our mission of making, maturing, and missioning disciples?

3. Are we willing to invest in the things that we have deemed critical to the success of our mission?

4. Are we willing to *not* do things, even very good things, for the sake of priorities that need to happen in order to move the growth and mission forward?

You can download a free copy of these questions, as well as an overview of the Take a Leap process, by going to **http:// m3catholic.com/take-a-leap.**

Acknowledgements

I'm always amazed at the work it takes to turn an idea into a book. Behind every successful published manuscript stands a team of dedicated professionals who apply their talents, experience, and energy to help create something far greater than the author could produce alone.

The team surrounding me from The Word Among Us Press is one of the best I have ever worked with. Every person who touched this book in some way—whether from editorial, production, finance, logistics, or warehousing—made it possible for you, the reader, to experience it. If you find this work helpful or fruitful in any way, the folks at The Word Among Us Press deserve the credit.

The themes and processes in this book emerged out of twenty-plus years of work in the areas of evangelization, parish renewal, and organizational leadership. I am grateful and indebted to my colleagues and friends who have also labored in these areas—especially Kristin Bird, Maureen Anderson, and Steve Anderson from Burning Hearts Disciples; Marcel LeJeune from Catholic Missionary Disciples; Tim Glemkowski from L'Alto Catholic Institute; Sherry Weddell and Katherine Coolidge from the Catherine of Siena Institute; and Matt Marchesci from FOCUS.

I have also been inspired, challenged, influenced, and formed by the often unsung work of my peers who give of themselves at the diocesan and parish level throughout the world—especially Bob Alexander, Shannon Ausloos, Joe Bland, Jennifer Brown, Linda

ABLAZE

Couri, Samantha Denefe, Rachel Espinoza, Michael "Gomer" Gormley, Mary Hallman, Kurt Klement, Tanya LeRue Noye, Fr. Ed Pelrine, Corey Robinson, Eleanor Segraves, Catherine Sims, Nancy Schmitt, Julianne Stanz, Marta Stepniak, John Stevens, Zara Tan, Bobby Vidal, Sr. Marie Kolbe Zamora, and others too numerous to name.

In the corporate world, I have benefited from the men and women who challenged, encouraged, collaborated with, and mentored me, including Peter Adkison, Linda Beardslee, Jim Butler, Ryan Dancey, Kelley Eskridge, Joe Hauck, Steve Horvath, Mark Jordan, Erik Mona, Luke Peterschmidt, Cindi Rice, Lisa Stevens, Anthony Valterra, Steve Winter, and David Wise, among others.

In a special way, I want to thank the parishes who have invited me to walk with them as a partner in this process of renewal and transformation—in particular Pam Lynch, Judy Reilly, Fr. David Ryan, Pam Urban, and the people of St. Francis de Sales' Parish in Lake Zurich, Illinois; Fr. Dan Hoehn, Sean Lazzari, and the community of St. Michael's Parish in Wheaton, Illinois; and Fr. Allan F. Wolfe, Pat Hallock, Denise Ziegler, and the people of St. Joseph's Parish in Lancaster, Pennsylvania. This book would not have been possible without your willingness to travel together on this journey.

A special thank you goes to Fr. Matt Bozovsky, Samantha Denefe, Rachel Espinoza, and Zara Tan, who looked over early versions of this manuscript and made important contributions to the final text.

Finally, past experience has shown that I can be a bit "testy" when I am in the midst of the writing process. Therefore my deepest gratitude goes to my wife, Debbie, and my daughter, Siena, for their love and support and for not allowing me to simply sit in my office and growl all day. I treasure the gift of our family!

Notes

1. *Lumen Gentium* [Dogmatic Constitution on the Church], 1, in Austin Flannery, OP, *Vatican Council II, Volume 1: The Conciliar and Post Conciliar Documents*, rev. ed. (New York: Costello, 1996), 350.
2. *Catechism of the Catholic Church*, 776, quoting *Lumen Gentium* 9, 48; *Gaudium et Spes* [On the Church in the Modern World] 45; Paul VI, June 22, 1973; *Ad Gentes* [Missionary Activity of the Church] 7; cf. *Lumen Gentium* 17.
3. Diocese of Westminster, "Sacraments," https://rcdow.org.uk/att/files/faith/catechesis/baptism/sacraments.pdf.
4. See Sherry Weddell, *Forming Intentional Disciples: The Path to Knowing and Following Jesus* (Huntington, IN: Our Sunday Visitor, 2012); Fr. James Mallon, *Divine Renovation: Bringing Your Parish From Maintenance to Mission* (New London, CT: Twenty-Third Publications, 2014); Michael White and Tom Corcoran, *Rebuilt: Awakening the Faithful, Reaching the Lost, and Making Church Matter* (Notre Dame, IN: Ave Maria Press, 2013).
5. Pope Paul VI, *Evangelii Nuntiandi* [On Evangelization in the Modern World], 14, http://w2.vatican.va/content/paul-vi/en/apost_exhortations/documents/hf_p-vi_exh_19751208_evangelii-nuntiandi.html.
6. Weddell, 11.
7. Edgar Schein with Peter Scheen, *Organizational Culture and Leadership*, 5th ed. (Hoboken, NJ: John Wiley & Sons, 2017), 6.

8. Fr. Simon Lobo, CC, *Divine Renovation Apprentice: Learning to Lead a Disciple-Making Parish* (Frederick, MD: The Word Among Us Press, 2018), 19.

9. Roger Connors and Tom Smith, *Change the Culture, Change the Game: The Breakthrough Strategy for Energizing Your Organization and Creating Accountability for Results* (New York: Portfolio/Penguin, 2012), 57.

10. *Culture Hacker* podcast, 2017, season 1, episode 4. On-air talent includes Michelle Crosby and Shane Green.

11. Schein and Scheen, 6.

12. See Connors and Smith, 7.

13. Alzheimer's Association, https://www.alz.org/.

14. Strategic Management Insight, https://www.strategicmanagementinsight.com/mission-statements/target-mission-statement.html.

15. Albert Winseman, *Growing An Engaged Church: How to Stop "Doing Church and Start Being the Church Again* (New York: Gallup Press, 2006), 28.

16. Fr. James Mallon, *Divine Renovation: Bringing Your Parish From Maintenance to Mission* (New London, CT: Twenty Third Publications, 2014), 150.

17. Gil Rendle, *Doing the Math of Mission: Fruits, Faithfulness, and Metrics* (London: Rowman and Littlefield, 2014), 14.

18. Quoted by Fr. Thomas Berg, "Evangelii Gaudium: Exhorting a Self-referential Church," Catholic News Agency, December 5, 2013, https://www.catholicnewsagency.com/column/evangelii-gaudium-exhorting-a-self-referential-church-2753.

19. William Sloane Coffin, *Credo* (Louisville, KY: Westminster John Knox Press, 2004), 140-141.

20. Rendle, 20-21.

21. Pope Francis, *Evangelii Gaudium* [On the Proclamation of the Gospel in Today's World], 27, http://w2.vatican.va/content/francesco/en/apost_exhortations/documents/papa-francesco_esortazione-ap_20131124_evangelii-gaudium.html.

22. Banning Liebscher, *Jesus Culture: Calling a Generation to Revival* (Shippensburg, PA: Destiny Image Publishers 2015), 54-55.

24. Sherry Weddell, *Fruitful Discipleship: Living the Mission of Jesus in the Church and the World* (Huntington, IN: Our Sunday Visitor, 2017), 216.

25. Ibid., 217.

26. Ibid., 217.

27. *Divine Renovation: An Interview with Fr. James Mallon*, part 4, https://youtu.be/hNw5xvTfe0s.

28. Patrick Lencioni, *The Advantage: Why Organizational Health Trumps Everything Else in Business* (San Francisco: Jossey-Bass, 2012), 3.

29. Peter Bromberg, "Purposeful Influence," Keynote presentation at the Connecticut Library Leadership Institute, West Hartford, CT, August 9, 2013.

30. See Kim Scott, *Radical Candor: Be a Kick-Ass Boss Without Losing Your Humanity* (New York: St. Martin's Press, 2017), especially chapter 1.

31. Lencioni, 38

32. Scott, 9.

33. Lencioni, 38.

34. Patty Azzarello, *Move: How Decisive Leaders Execute Strategy Despite Obstacles, Setbacks, & Stalls* (Hoboken, NJ: John Wiley & Sons, 2017), Introduction.

35. Keith Strohm, "Praying it Forward: Intercession and the Transformation of Your Parish," in Sherry Weddell, ed., *Becoming a Parish of Intentional Disciples* (Huntington, IN: Our Sunday Visitor, 2015), 32.

36. Ken Kamen, "The Financial Wisdom of Yogi Berra," Forbes Online, September 24, 2015, www.forbes.com/sites/investor/2015/09/24/the-financial-wisdom-of-yogi-berra-2.
37. Lencioni, 82.
38. Lencioni, 91.
39. Connors and Smith, 115.
40. Lencioni, 94.
41. Connors and Smith, 26.
42. Larry Bossidy and Ram Charan, *Confronting Reality: Doing What Matters to Get Things Right* (New York: Crown Business, 2004), 195-196.
43. Connors and Smith, 121.
44. Mallon, 182-83.
45. Keith Strohm, *The 10 Biggest Lies of the Enemy—And How to Combat Them* (Frederick, MD: The Word Among Us Press, 2018), 94.
46. Excerpt from Deacon Keith Strohm, *Jesus: The Story You Thought You Knew* (Huntington, IN: Our Sunday Visitor, 2013), 143-144. Used by permission. No other use of this material is authorized.
47. Weddell, *Forming Intentional Disciples,* 65.

About the Author

Deacon Keith Strohm is the former director of the Office for the New Evangelization and a deacon for the Archdiocese of Chicago. Deacon Keith has extensive experience in creating and sustaining processes and programs of evangelization and formation at the group, parish, and diocesan levels that focus on the making, maturation, and missioning of disciples of Jesus Christ. A sought-after international speaker and conference keynote, he has helped tens of thousands of men and women hear the gospel message and encounter the mercy, love, and power of Jesus Christ. Deacon Keith is also the executive director of M3 Ministries (www.m3catholic.com) and a contributing author for Sherry Weddell's book, *Becoming a Parish of Intentional Disciples*, a follow-up to the bestselling book, *Forming Intentional Disciples*. Deacon Keith has published two other books—*Jesus: The Story You Thought You Knew* and *The 10 Biggest Lies of the Enemy—And How to Combat Them*. You can follow him on Twitter (@KeithStrohm).

About M3 Ministries

M3 Ministries provides proven, practical formation, coaching, and events for Catholics and church leaders at all levels designed to help build communities that make, mature, and mission (send out) disciples of Jesus Christ. We organically equip parishes and dioceses with the tools and support needed to change culture and create missionary communities that bear fruit in the twenty-first century.

Even the best tools, processes, and programs will only get you so far. Real, lasting parish transformation occurs when we begin to intentionally live out the supernatural dimensions of life in Christ and combine them with solid leadership, clear strategy, commitment, and fruitful processes. This is the foundation of our approach at M3 Ministries. We integrate our deep understanding of evangelization, practical experience with leading and training organizations, and our concrete knowledge of making disciples with the power of the Holy Spirit and the spiritual riches given to the Church to raise up missionary leaders capable of nurturing and supporting a culture of mission and discipleship at the parish and diocesan levels.

Whether you are looking for specific training in evangelization, an evangelizing event (such as a parish mission or retreat), or longer-term accompaniment in the development of missionary leaders and the transformation of your parish or diocese, we can help. To learn more about M3 Ministries, visit m3catholic. com or email Deacon Keith Strohm at keith@m3catholic.com.